By Bruce Holdt:

Brazil

Murder in San Francisco

Gunboats Forever

BRAZIL

BRUCE HOLDT

BRAZIL

Library of Congress Control Number: 2013914475
ISBN: Hardcover   978-1-4836-8374-4
                 Softcover   978-1-4836-8373-7
                 eBook   978-1-4836-8375-1

Rev. date: 01/31/2014

You may buy books by Bruce Holdt at:
www.BruceHoldt.com
542860

CONTENTS

PIRATES 9

INTRODUCTION 15

CHAPTER 1: LANGUAGE TRAINING.............................17
CHAPTER 2: DIA TRAINING 23
CHAPTER 3: CIA TRAINING 25
CHAPTER 4: OUR ARRIVAL IN RIO.................................29
CHAPTER 5: RIO DE JANEIRO 45
CHAPTER 6: CRIME IN RIO 69
CHAPTER 7: GREGORIA..72
CHAPTER 8: BRAZILIAN NAVY 76
CHAPTER 9: ANTONIO FERRER 83
CHAPTER 10: TONY'S AGED CACHAÇA 88
CHAPTER 11: BOUZIOS 90
CHAPTER 12: PARATY 95
CHAPTER 13: CAPRI 100
CHAPTER 14: MUSSEL ISLAND.......................................102
CHAPTER 15: BRASILIA..105
CHAPTER 16: RECIFE SHIP VISIT....................................116
CHAPTER 17: AIRCRAFT CARRIER VISIT 120
CHAPTER 18: ATTACHÉ TRIP 129
CHAPTER 19: SOUTHERN BRAZIL...................................140
CHAPTER 20: THE US ATTACHES 154
CHAPTER 21: RIO'S RESTAURANTS 160
CHAPTER 22: YIPEE PARK..168
CHAPTER 23: MONKEY RESTAURANT...........................176
CHAPTER 24: CIA..181
CHAPTER 25: THE ARTIST..202
CHAPTER 26: THE POSTMASTER 212
CHAPTER 27: THE WEDDING 215
CHAPTER 28: THE AMAZON 223
CHAPTER 29: COLUMBIA..239
CHAPTER 30: RETURN TO BRAZIL..................................244

ABOUT THE AUTHOR..247

This book is dedicated to my grandchildren, Ericka and Ethan Franze, Jacob, and Nathan Rowe, my pride and joy

Pirates

Karen and I decided to invite my good friend, Tony Ferrer and his wife, Francesca, to dinner one evening. When they arrived, Tony handed me his .45 that he always carried. I locked it in my desk drawer.

Below is a photograph I took of Tony and his wife on their yacht.

We invited them to join us on our balcony for appetizers and drinks. Gregoria had made Peruvian Pisco sours, which were Tony's favorite drink. She served nice Brazilian chardonnay for Karen and Francesca. Gregoria also served us grilled prawns and escargot for appetizers.

We talked for a while. "Bruce, would you and Karen like to join me on a cruise to the port of Santos? I have some business there next week."

"Of course, thank you for inviting us. I don't know much about Santos."

"You should. It is the port city for São Paulo. All imports to São Paulo pass through the port. It is one of the busiest ports in the world."

"When do we leave?"

"Nine tomorrow morning at the Yacht Club."

"We will be there before nine."

Below i s photograph of Tony and his wife.

When we boarded Tony's large beautiful motor yacht, Tony said, "Karen, have a seat on the afterdeck. Rodrigues will bring you a glass of wine. Bruce, come below with me."

We climbed down to the master suite. Tony always gave his master suite to Karen and me when we cruised with him. Tony opened a locked cabinet that was full of different kinds of weapons.

"Bruce, pick out a pistol and a rifle that you feel comfortable with."

I selected a .45 automatic, as I had been on a pistol team that shot only .45s

Below is a Photograph of the .45 automatic. (Wikipedia)

Then I selected an M-16 as I trained to us it earlier in my naval career. I also took several 30 round clips of ammunition for the rifle.

Below is a photograph of the M-16. (Wikipedia)

"What do I need the guns for?"

"We may need them, as there are pirates that operate out of several small ports near Santos. These pirates board yachts and kill the people on them. They then sell the yachts on the black market. Please put your guns in the drawer under your bed. I do not think you should tell Karen about this. It would just frighten her."

Welcome to Brazil, I thought.

About four hours later, "We will be in Santos in about an hour."

"Tony, do you see the boat rapidly approaching us off the starboard bow?"

"Yes, it is a cigarette boat. Go below and get your guns and plenty of ammunition. I think it is a pirate boat."

A cigarette boat is a small, fast boat designed with a long narrow platform and a planning hull to enable it to reach high speeds.

During prohibition, similar boats smuggled liquor from Canada into the United States. These boats got their name because the Italian Mafia use them to smuggle untaxed cigarettes from Northern Africa to Italia to sell in the black market.

"Bruce, when the boat gets within range, fire a clip at the cockpit. There are armed men in the cockpit!"

I had never shot another person in the twenty-eight years I had been in the Navy. I thought, *I have to shot them. I if I do not they will kill all of us.* I immediately switched the rifle to full automatic and fired an entire clip from my M-15 at the cockpit.

"Good shooting Bruce. You hit the pilot. The boat is slowing down. Quickly load another clip and empty it at the boat's waterline."

I ejected the empty clip and slammed a loaded one into the M-15. I pulled the trigger and held the fully automatic on the waterline of the cigarette boat.

"Way to go Bruce. The boat is sinking from your last M-15 barrage."

"Great. We got the bastards!"

Karen stuck her head out and walked out on the afterdeck. "Bruce, that was magnificent. I had no idea you could shoot like that! But why did you shoot at that boat?"

"They were pirates trying to board us. They would have killed all of us!"

"Wow, wait till I tell the kids!"

"You better not. We will never hear the end of it. They won't let us go on Tony's yacht ever again."

Introduction

I decided to write this book because I enjoyed my time in Brazil so much that I wanted to share it with others. Most Americans know very little about Brazil. For example, the majority of people in Latin America do not speak Spanish. They speak Portuguese. The population of Brazil is larger than the population of the other Latin American countries combined. The gross domestic product of Brazil is larger than all the rest of Latin America combined. In addition, the city of São Paulo, Brazil, has more people in it than the country of Argentina. São Paulo has the second largest population of all the cities in the world.

Some of the activities, I was involved with during my time as the Defense Attaché in Rio de Janeiro were highly classified. Because of this, I have changed the names of all US and Brazilian military personnel and members of the CIA in the book. I also have changed the description of classified activities to similar but somewhat different activities, to avoid revealing any still classified information.

The events in this book took place over 25 years ago, so I may have forgotten some of the details about the events I describe in my book.

Chapter 1: Language Training

In the summer of 1987, while working in the Office of the Chief of Naval Personnel, I decided that I wanted to get out of the rat race in Washington, DC, and travel outside the US. I requested an assignment as a defense attaché.

My detailer gave me three choices for an attaché assignment. They were Belgrade, Yugoslavia, Santiago, Chile, or Rio de Janeiro, Brazil. I was not interested in Yugoslavia because of the turmoil there. However, Chile interested me, until I found out two American teenagers were doused with gasoline and set on fire in Santiago, during an anti-government demonstration. Rio became my first choice.

Prior to going to Brazil, I received a year of Brazilian language training at the State Department Foreign Language Institute in Rosslyn, VA.

Marissa, one of my language teachers had red hair and did not look like a Brazilian like the other teachers.

I asked Marissa about her red hair. She told me she was from a small town in Southern Brazil that her German ancestors settled in after the Second World War. Her husband, born in Germany, required Marissa and their two boys to only speak German at home. Marissa taught the boys to speak Portuguese and English. By the time they started school, the boys were already fluent in the three languages.

My language class had only four students. The other three students were career Foreign Service Officers, who had assignments to the US Embassy in Brasilia, Brazil.

The language instruction included a one-on-one session every day. I was able to request Marissa for the session. She was very patient with my mispronunciations of words and my bad grammar. When I had trouble with a lesson, she would stay after class and coach me on the lesson, until I had learned it. Primarily, because of Marissa's professional skills, I learned to speak Portuguese fairly well.

While I was in Language school, my family lived in our home next to my mother in law's home in a small town in Northern Minnesota. I lived in Bachelor Officers' Quarters (BOQ) in US Naval Support Activity Anacostia, Virginia, a suburb of Washington, DC.

The BOQ was on the Columbia River. I decided to try my hand at fishing. I bought a rod and reel and some bait. I casted the bait into the river while standing on it grassy bank. The only fish I caught was one catfish. I filleted the fish and fried one fillet. It tasted awful, so I stopped fishing in the dirty river.

Below is a photograph of a catfish.

The Officer's Club next to the BOQ had a band every Wednesday night that imitated the Blues Brothers. I had to go early to get a seat at the bar to watch the show. I would order a sandwich and a beer, so I had something to do until the band arrived and started playing. They were scheduled to play three separate sets but always ended up playing. The club was always full for the show. We all had a great time.

Once a week, the students and teachers in the Brazilian section of the language school would bring a dish from their native country. I to make bruschetta, a dish of toasted Italian bread slices with a tapenade of tomatoes, green onions, garlic, and olive oil. I had learned to make bruschetta when we lived in Italy.

Below is a photograph of the bruschetta.

When I made the toast in the BOQ, I put several pieces of bread into a large toaster. While I was busy chopping tomatoes and onions and not watching the toaster, the bread began to burn and smoke. The smoke set off the fire alarm. We had to evacuate the entire BOQ, until the firefighters had arrived in two fire trucks to put out the fire that caused the alarm BOQ fire alarms. I did not tell anyone that I set of the alarm by making toast, but it was a great story for my classmates as they ate my bruschetta.

One the weekends I worked for a local company that took children and teenagers skiing. We rode buses from Washington, DC, to a variety of mountains in Virginia, West Virginia, and New York.

I enjoyed skiing with older, better skiers as they did not need a lot of instruction. I also skied with another instructor, a CIA agent who had taught the Greek Army to ski. He skied on long skis in the Austrian skiing style. I bought a pair of extra-long skis like his. To this day, I am comfortable with only these skis.

Below is a photo another instructor took of me showing the teenagers above how to traverse a steep slope.

Skiing every weekend helped me lose twenty pounds. By the end of the skiing season, I was in great shape. I weighed 180 pounds, exactly what I weighed when I graduated from high school.

In order to get around DC, I bought a beat up 1963 Fiat convertible, which was literally falling apart. I used the Special Services Garage on the Support Activity Anacostia to repair the various things wrong with the car. I even welded a sheet of aluminum to the floor of the car, which had a large hole in it. I also had to weld the front and back bumpers back together.

Below is a picture I took of my fiat.

The Fiat did not have a heater. On one snowy very cold winter day. On the drive back to Anacostia from the language school. I became so cold that I drove off the main road in Alexandria, Virginia, towards the Metro Station. I drove as far as I could and parked the car alongside the street in a snow bank. I walked to the Metro and took it back to Anacostia.

A few days later, I took the metro to Alexandria. I found the Fiat parked almost perpendicular to the sidewalk. I was lucky not to get a parking ticket.

Chapter 2: DIA Training

After language school, I attended Military Attaché Training at the Defense Intelligence Agency (DIA) on the Bolling Air Force base next to the Naval Support Activity.

Below is a photograph of DIA Headquarters.

The DIA is the producer and manager of foreign military intelligence information for the United States. As one of the principal members of the US intelligence community, the agency works to support national-level defense objectives for the president, the secretary of defense, and senior US military and civilian policymakers.

DIA work encompasses all aspects of military intelligence requirements, including defense-related foreign political, economic, industrial, geographic, and medical and health intelligence. Further,

DIA leads the intelligence community in collection and production of measurement and signature intelligence.

I was as part of The DIA clandestine military attaché service. We conducted espionage activities around the world, particularly in countries, like Brazil, where the Department of Defense (DOD) has better access or more foreign militaries than the Central Intelligence Agency (CIA).

A military attaché is a military expert, attached to a diplomatic mission. Military attachés are usually high-ranking military officers who retain their commissions, while serving in an embassy or consulate. Opportunities also sometimes arise for military attachés to serve in the field with military forces of another state.

Military attaché training includes methods for collecting clandestine intelligence information, photography, and press interviews. I had a practice press interview with an actual television news interviewer.

"Commander Holdt, how do you intend to speak to Brazilians? Do you speak Spanish?"

"No. I speak Portuguese."

It was clear he had no idea that Portuguese was the official language of Brazil. Actually, the interviewer was unaware of many facts about Brazil as most Americans are. For example, most people do not know that the majority of Latin America do not speak Spanish; they speak Portuguese.

Chapter 3: CIA Training

Part of my attaché training was three weeks of training with the CIA at one of their secret, remote locations. I am not sure where but it was in Virginia, maybe even the CIA's notorious "Farm'.

The first training phase was automobile training, however unlike any automobile training that, you have ever heard of. The CIA had built a paved rectangle about the size of a football field and a paved racetrack. There were about twenty cars parked at one end of the paved area. Some of them were wrecks. Others looked like souped-up police cars.

Our CIA trainer said, "The first phase of the training will be on the racetrack. There will be a lead car, and you will be in the second car, following the lead car. I want you to stay on the tail of the lead car, nearly touching it, no matter how fast it goes. It will be easy to do that on the straight ways. However, the curves will be much harder. Just remember the following. Start the turns as close to the inside of the track at a steady speed. About halfway through the turn, floor it right out of the turn."

When my turn finally came, I was very excited. I had some stock racing as a teenager and was confident I would do well. I stayed on the tail of the lead car around the track. When the lead car sped up, I increased the speed of my car, staying on his tail, nudging the lead car with my bumper.

After the third nudge, the instructor sitting beside me said, "Bruce, you did great, but let's pull in now. That's all I can take."

I looked at the instructor, and my driving had obviously shaken him. He never rode with me again, throughout the rest of the driving training. He must have gotten sick and gone home, as I never saw him again.

The next automobile training was called the "Roadblock Crash." They set up a roadblock, consisting of two wrecked cars pushed together with their bumpers touching. The instructor said, "You will get in the crash car and try to crash through the simulated roadblock, by driving directly at the center of the two cars."

I was third in line and was able to observe the first two trainees as they tried to crash through the barrier. Both of them had to take three runs at the roadblock until they were able to crash through it. I thought, *They are going much too slow to break through. I am going to go much faster when it is my turn.*

I got in the car and the Instructor said, "Start at the yellow line there. You are on your own. Let's see what you can do."

I floored the car and hit the roadblock at 70 miles an hour. My car blew the two cars completely apart and barely slowed at all. After I drove back to the waiting line and got out of the car, the instructor smiled and said, "Good job. That is the way you are supposed to do it."

The next of the automobile training was the "Quick Reversal." The instructor said, "To complete what we call the "Quick Reversal," you will drive the car at about 60 miles an hour, pull the emergency brake on full, slam down the brake pedal, and turn the steering wheel completely to the left. The car will start a hard skid to the left. As you are nearing the e of the skid, release the parking brake, take your foot off the brake pedal, and straighten out the steering wheel.

If you do everything, I told you, the car will reverse direction with little loss of speed. This is the best way to lose a car following you. The following car driver is usually surprised by your maneuver and will pass by you and be unable to reverse direction in time to catch up to you.

The instructor said, "Bruce, since you did so well on the roadblock exercise, you go first."

I followed the instructions, as best I could, and was able to complete the exercise successfully.

The second phase of the CIA was weapons training. We received training on many kinds of handheld weapons, revolvers, and automatics. As I had been on a .45 automatic pistol team earlier in my career, I did best on it.

We then fired different kinds of rifles, including the M-15 and M-16, several different machine guns, and shotguns. I liked the Israeli Uzi the best among the machine guns. I did the best on a sawed-off 12-gauge shotgun.

Below is a photograph of the Uzi.

The next phase of the training was hand-to-hand combat. Since I had been on the wrestling team in high school and a judo team in college and in the Navy, I was looking forward to the training. Master Inoki was our instructor. He taught the mixed martial arts, which is a full-contact combat sport that uses the best techniques of all the martial arts, including karate, judo, jujitsu, and tae kwon do.

I learned quickly and became quite adept by the end of the session. I never had to use my skills in hand-to-hand combat. However, the training gave me the confidence to enter into some very tight situations as an attaché.

Chapter 4: Our Arrival in Rio

After over a year of training, we packed our bags and flew to Rio de Janeiro. The current Defense Attaché, Air Force Major Gary Richter, and the Naval Attaché LCDR Timothy Atkinson met us at the airport. I would be relieving Gary as the Military Attaché in Rio de Janeiro.

The fact that there are military attachés in Rio is due to the history of changing the capital of Brazil from Rio de Janeiro to Brasília. Brasília is in the center of Brazil. The Americans agreed to keep US Military Attachés in Rio at the insistence of the Brazilian military.

Below is a photograph I took of the front of the US Consulate.

We were very tired after the long flight, so LCDR Atkinson took us to a nice hotel for the night. However, it was very noisy because of the constant traffic outside the hotel. Therefore, we moved to the Hideaway Hotel, which was located a good distance from any traffic.

Below is a photograph of the Hideaway Hotel

The hotel was only one block from the Leme Beach, one of the cleanest beaches in Rio. We went the beach every weekend and often in the evenings to watch the sun set. There were food stands on the beach, so we could buy something to eat and drink. Young boys towed ice chests on small wagons and sold beer and soft drinks. We would often stay on the beach until it was time to go to bed.

Below is a photograph of Leme Beach.

The hotel was near two very good restaurants. Shirley's was one of the restaurants. It was a tiny seafood restaurant. Shirley's was normally very busy. However, they always seemed to have room for us. Our favorite dish at Shirley's were large charbroiled prawns served on a skewer hanging from a crossbar over your plate. Since Brazil has no kelp beds for shrimps to feed on, the large shrimps or prawns taste like lobsters.

The other restaurant was Michael's Churrascaria, a Churrascaria. A Churrascaria is a restaurant that charbroils all kinds of meats, including beef, lamb, chicken, and pork, over a large wood fire on long skewers. Waiters bring the meat to your table on the skewer, and off thin slices onto your plate.

Because it is so hot in most parts of Brazil, ranchers raise Indo-Brazilian cattle of a Zebu beef breed developed in Brazil from Cattle brought from India. Indo-Brazilian cattle have good heat and parasite resistance and thrive in the tropics. They are white to dark grey in colour with short horns and very large ears. They have the typical Zebu shoulder hump.

Below is a photograph I took of some Brazilian cattle.

On each table is a small piece of wood shaped like an hourglass, which has a red and a green end. When the green end is showing, it means someone at your table wants more meat. If the red end is showing, no one at the table wants more.

Below is a Photograph of the skewers of meat as they cooked on the grill.

Michael's has also had a buffet with a large variety of seafood and salads. There was cold lobster, oysters on the half shell, mussels, crab, shrimp, salmon, and a variety of olives, salads. Fresh fruit. I had to be careful not to eat too much of the seafood so I would have room some of the meat.

My family would not visit the buffet as they were always much more interested in starting right out with the meats. I would often just have a plate of the chicken hearts, which was my favorite.

We made up stories about chicken hearts when we would return to the United States. One story was that I would kill so many chickens to get their hearts that dead chickens covered the roads near to our home.

Below is a photograph of the buffet

The Churrascarias always served a drink called a Caipirinha.

Below is a photo I took of a Caipirinha on our table

To make a Caipirinha you: Cut a lime into eight pieces; remove all seeds and the white core. Put the lime pieces in a whisky glass, and add three teaspoons of sugar. Crush the lime and sugar with a wooden pestle. Fill the glass with crushed ice, lime, and sugar up to one inch from the rim. Pour cachaça over the mixture and enjoy.

Below are the things you need to make a Caipirinha.

They are best when made with raw sugar.

We spent several days trying to find a place to live. We had planned to take LCDR Atkinson's apartment, however when we saw it we did not like it at all.

My allowance for housing was quite substantial. We could afford to rent just about any home in Rio. We wanted to be close to the beach. However, all the apartments on the beach were too small.

Our real estate agent showed us an apartment that was located in Leme, near the Lagoa. The Lagoa is a large lake surrounded by nice homes and apartments. We took one look and knew it was the one for us. It was by far the nicest home we had seen. I requested a meeting with the owner to negotiate a rental price.

The real estate agent said, "That is easy. The owner lives in the building on the top floor, he is an American expatriate. He and his wife spend half of the year in Brazil and the other half in Florida. He owns a beautiful home in Key Largo. He is a retired physician. Let's take the elevator up to his apartment."

We took the elevator to his apartment. "Commandante and Senhora Holdt I would like to present Doctor Steve Van Hee and his wife Rita."

Doctor Van Hee responded in English. "I am happy to meet you please come in and have a seat."

"Thank you Doctor, We like the apartment and would like to rent it."

"Good. That calls for some champagne. It nearly five PM so I am sure Commander that you are off duty."

"Champagne will be great. Thank you."

We sat down and their maid brought us champagne.

"To get right to the point, I would like to know how much the rent for the apartment is."

"I have to quote it in Brazilian currency, as Brazilian law does not allow me to collect any rent in dollars, as much as I would like to. We just switched from crusados to reals. I need to use my calculator to convert the previous rent from crusados to reals. The government thinks that switching currency will stop the inflation. However, I know it will not."

He quoted me a figure in reals that equaled about $1,500 a month. I was prepared to pay at least $2,000. A similar apartment would easily cost $5,000 in most American cities.

"We accept."

"Good, now we will have three Americans living here. John and Elizabeth Anderson rent he third floor apartment. They both work in the Cultural Affairs office in the US Consulate."

"Then we will have a little community of American's here. I have not met the Anderson's yet." I knew that the John Anderson was the CIA Chief of Station. His wife, Virginia, also was with the CIA. However, I could not tell Steve that as the CIA was very careful not to reveal the identity of their agents in Brazil.

Our apartment filled the fifth floor of the six-story apartment building. It had a large kitchen, a dining room, four bedrooms, and a long balcony. We always ate breakfast on the balcony and dinner in the dining room.

Below is a photograph of the Lagoa. Our apartment was on the small strip of land between the Lagoa and the Atlantic Ocean.

Our apartment was larger than most houses we had lived in. Each of us had a spacious bed and attached bathroom. The living room was so large we had three couches in it and it had a fireplace that we never had the opportunity to use.

Furniture for the apartment came from a furniture warehouse owned by the US Consulate. We visited and picked out the furniture we wanted to have in our apartment. The next day, it the consulate workers delivered the furniture to our apartment. Everything we needed was furnished by the consulate. We only brought our clothes and a set of china and Waterford crystal for entertaining our dinner guests.

The balcony was large enough so that we were able to seat thirty-two members of the consulate staff and admirals from the Brazilian navy and a general from the Brazilian Marine Corps. The consulate furnished six dining tables and chairs and the silverware, dishes, and linen for the tables

Below is a drawing of our apartment.

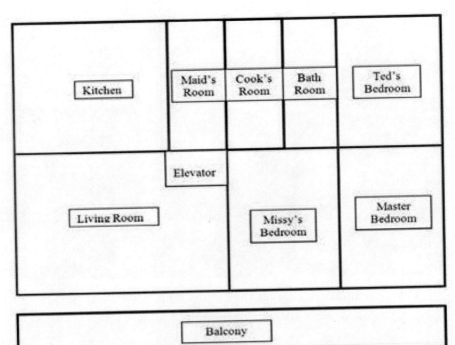

Below is a photo of Ted and I sitting in our living room. Behind is a large table on our balcony we used for eating breakfast.

Below is a photo I took of Karen enjoying a glass of wine on our balcony one Fourth of July.

The inflation was so high in Brazil that I always paid my rent on the last day of the month. I called a person whose phone number I received from Major Richter. I would tell him that I wanted to purchase the Brazilians reals that I had agreed to pay for rent. He would tell me the amount in dollars for the reals.

A few minutes later, I was called to the lobby of the consulate. A messenger handed me a brown paper bag full of reals and I gave him an envelope of dollars.

I then called my driver to my office and handed him the bag of reals. He then drove to the office of my real estate agent and handed him the bag of reals for the rent for my apartment. Each month the rent got cheaper and cheaper. By the time we left Brazil, it was down to $700 dollars from the original $1,500.

Food and drink in the local bars and restaurants was also very inexpensive. A draft beer in most bars was only 10 cents. I could buy a meal for my family for $12 in a nearby non-tourist restaurant.

One of our favorite local restaurants served a plate with a half of chicken that was flattened, grilled, and served with French fries and a delicious salad of sliced tomatoes, onions, and hearts of palm, dressed in olive oil. The typical tourist restaurants were more expensive. However, I could still buy a dinner and drinks for the four of us for around $30 dollars.

Food in the market was also very inexpensive. Gregoria, our maid shopped every morning for the day's meals before breakfast. We had fresh baked small loaves of French bread delivered to our apartment every morning. Every two weeks a deliveryman brought two cases of beer and one case of wine to our apartment. Expatriate Germans, who had immigrated to southern Brazil after World War II, brewed all of the beers I liked. Italian families, who had come with the Germans, made the wine.

Major Richter told us the Brazilian government would bug our telephone in our apartment. The day after we moved in, my wife was standing on our balcony.

"Bruce, come here."

"Yes, what do you want?"

"What are those men down there doing? They are digging up the street in front of our apartment building."

"I think they are bugging our phone."

From then on, when we answered our phones, we would hear a loud click, meaning somebody was listening. I made any calls of a classified nature on my secure phone in my consulate office.

Every morning Karen and I would get up early and run around the Lagoa near our apartment. It was about a three-mile run. On weekends, the city government closed the road along the Leblon Beach to vehicle traffic. Every Sunday we would run on the closed road along the beach.

Below is a photograph of the Leblon Beach road on a Sunday.

We also enjoyed the Tijuca National Park for walking, which was located near a short drive from our apartment. Tijuca National Park is the largest city-surrounded urban forest and the second largest urban forest in the entire world. The park is a mountainous hand-planted rainforest in the city Proper of Rio It is a mountainous region, which encompasses the Tijuca Massif.

The Tijuca Forest is home to hundreds of species of plants and wildlife, many threatened by extinction, found only in the Atlantic Rainforest. All the original rainforest was destroyed to make way for coffee farms. In the second half of the 19th century in a successful effort to protect Rio's water supply.

Below are several photographs we took of the park.

Chapter 5: Rio de Janeiro

Since most of the rest of the book takes place in and around Rio de Janeiro, I would like to provide you readers with a little background information about Rio so you can better picture in your minds what occurs in the book as you read on.

Rio de Janeiro, commonly referred to simply as Rio, is the capital city of the state of Rio de Janeiro, the second largest city of Brazil, and the third largest metropolitan area and agglomeration in South America.

Rio is located on a strip of Brazil's Atlantic coast, close to the Tropic of Capricorn, where the shoreline is oriented east-west and face largely south. Portuguese settlers founded Rio on Guanabara Bay (Baía de Guanabara), an inlet on the coast.

Below is a photograph of the Harbor of Rio. The US Consulate is the tallest building in the right of the photo.

Cariocas is a Brazilian word that refers to the native inhabitants of Rio. The word comes from the indigenous language of the Tupi people living there, meaning "white man's house."

Rio was the capital of Brazil for nearly two centuries, from 1763 to 1815. During the Portuguese colonial era, from 1815 to 1821, Rio was the capital of the United Kingdom of Portugal, Brazil, and the Algarves from 1822 to 1960, an independent nation. Rio is nicknamed the Cidade

Below is a view of Rio de Janeiro at night.

The most popular attraction of Corcovado Mountain is the statue and viewing platform at its peak, drawing over 300,000 visitors per year. From the peak's platform the panoramic view includes downtown Rio, Sugarloaf Mountain, the Lagoa, Copacabana and Ipanema beaches, Estádio do Maracanã (Maracanã Stadium), and several of Rio's *favelas*. The view from Corcovado is spectacular. You can see all of the city of Rio, Sugar Loaf, many of Rio's beaches and even the city of Niteroi.

Below is an Ariel photograph of Rio taken from behind of Corcovado.

Copacabana, located in the southern zone of the city of Rio de Janeiro, Brazil, is known for its three-mile beach, one of the most famous beaches in the world. It is usually crowed with tourists. Many hotels, restaurants, bars, nightclubs and residential buildings dot the promenade along the beach. The Copacabana promenade is a paved sidewalk. Three miles long, it was completed in 1970 and has used a black and white Portuguese pavement design since its origin in the 1930s: a geometric wave.

Below is a photograph I took of Copacabana Beach.

The Copacabana Palace Hotel is the most famous and luxurious hotel in Rio de Janeiro, Brazil. It is South America's premier hotel, having received the rich and famous for the past 80 years. It faces the Copacabana Beach. It consists of an 8-story main building and a 14-story annex. French architect Joseph Gire designed the hotel. It has 216 rooms (148 in the main building and 78 in the annex), an— Olympic swimming pool, an exclusive swimming pool for VIP guests located at the penthouse, a tennis court, fitness center, a 3-story spa, two bars, a nightclub and two restaurants. Inaugurated on August 13, 1923, After Brasília became the Brazilian capital in 1960, the hotel underwent a period of slow decline, and the more modern hotels, built in the 1970s, surpassed it. There were plans to demolish the hotel in 1985. However, the Orient Express group bought the hotel and refurbished it.

Below is a photograph of the Copacabana Palace Hotel

Every December 31, 2.5 million people gather at Copacabana Beach to celebrate New Year's in Rio de Janeiro. The crowd, mostly dressed in white, celebrates all night at the hundreds of different shows and events along the beach. It is the second largest celebration only next to the Carnival. People celebrat+e the New Year by sharing chilled champagne. It is considered good luck to shake the champagne bottle and spray around at midnight. Chilled champagne adds to the spirit of the festivities. New Year's Eve in Rio is spectacular. All the Brazilians dress totally in white and gather on the beaches of Rio. Many of the hotels along the beaches shoot of magnificent fireworks from their rooftops.

We enjoyed watching the revelers from a friend's balcony. We were able to relax with a glass of champagne and watch the fireworks with many friends. It may have been the best New Year's Eve in my life. We took many photographs. The following photographs are just a few we too.

Below are photographs of the fireworks along Copacabana Beach.

Other local traditions include cleansing oneself in the ocean waters as well as throwing flowers and small mementos into the surf with the belief that if they do not come back, your wish or prayer will be granted.

Below is a Photograph the people in Copacabana on New Year's Eve

To the north of Leme and at the entrance to Guanabara Bay is the district of Urca and the Sugar Loaf Mountain (Pão de Açúcar), whose name describes the famous mountain rising out of the sea. Rising 1,299 ft. above the harbor, its name refers to its resemblance to the traditional shape of concentrated refined loaf of sugar.

A two-stage cable-car trip from Praia Vermelha carries passengers to the summit of Sugar Loaf with the intermediate stop on Morro da Urca. It offers views second only to Corcovado Mountain.

Below is a photograph of a cable car approaching Pão de Açúcar.

Corcovado, meaning "hunchback" in Portuguese, is a mountain in central Rio. The 2,329 ft. granite peak is located in the Tijuca Forest. Corcovado lies just west of the city center but is wholly within the city limits and visible from great distances. It is known worldwide for the 125 ft. statue of Jesus atop its peak, entitled *Cristo Redentor* or "Christ the Redeemer."

Below is a photograph of the Christ the Redeemer Statue.

Leme Beach was only two short blocks from our apartment. It was one of the cleanest beaches in Rio. In the winter months that the Brazilians think is very cold. At times in the winter, Karen and I were often the only people on the entire beach. Brazilians found this to be so interesting, they would stop, get out of their cars, and take photos of us.

Because we were on the beach during all of the seasons of the year, we became very tan and looked like Brazilians. Rio had frequent robberies of tourists. We dressed like Brazilians and never spoke English on the streets. I even had a fake throw away wallet that had a number of reals and expired credit cards to hand to any would be robber. I put one credit card and more reals in my front pocket. Luckily, I never had to turn over the wallet to a robber.

Below is a photograph of Leme beach in the height of the tourist season.

We found even a cleaner beach called Guaratiba, about an hour's drive south of Rio. It was a very beautiful secluded beach. There was no parking near the beach. We had to park nearby.

The beach had a great restaurant within walking distance that only served shrimp moqueca. The restaurant was small and run by an older Brazilian couple. Papa cooked food and Mama served the food. The moqueca was the best moqueca we had in Brazil. The shrimp was freshly caught and the vegetables, grown by the owners. We ate at the restaurant every time we visited Guaratiba Beach.

Below is a photograph of Guaratiba Beach taken from the restaurant.

Shrimp moqueca is a stew made of shrimps, red and green bell peppers, onions, garlic, and tomatoes, cooked in coconut and olive oil, and seasoned with fresh coriander and red pepper sauce.

Moqueca is a Brazilian seafood stew based on fish, onions, garlic, tomatoes, and cilantro. It is cooked slowly, with no water added. Brazilians have been making *moqueca* for at least 300 years.

Moqueca can be made with fish, shrimp, crabs, sea crab, or lobsters. There is also a rare variety made with raw bananas. The dish is seasoned with onion, tomatoes, cilantro, chives, and olive oil.

I liked moqueca and tried it wherever I traveled in Brazil. I still make moqueca today in Minnesota, having brought all the ingredients for it from Brazil. I can buy the ingredients now in stores specializing in foods from Latin America.

Below is a photo of a typical earthenware bowl of shrimp moqueca.

Later that year, Karen's sister Joan visited us for two weeks. She and Karen went shopping, and Joan bought a beautiful hand-crocheted white tablecloth. She put the tablecloth in the trunk of my car. I locked in the trunk when we went swimming at Guaratiba beach. When we returned to the car, its trunk was jimmied open, and the tablecloth was missing.

We took Joan to all of the beaches in Rio and to many of our favorite restaurants. She like Brazil so much that she decided to return with her husband the following year.

Pictured below are Joan and me sitting on Copacabana Beach.

On weekends, there were street fairs in front of the Copacabana Hotel. We often visited the street fairs. Many of the treasures we returned to the United States with we bought at one of the street fairs.

Below is a photo of Copacabana with the street fair in the background.

The numerous stands sold all kinds handmade Brazilian goods and carved wooden items, often made and sold by ingenious Indians.

Below is a typical stand selling Indian made goods.

On the western side of the street fair was a row of shops. Located in the middle was Star Jewelry. I recommended his jewelry store to all the US ships as Antonio guaranteed that he would not overprice his jewelry for any of the sailors who visited his shop. Because of this, he did very well every time a US ship visited Rio.

Missy wanted an aquamarine ring, as it was her birthstone. We visited Star Jewelry. Antonio brought out several beautiful aquamarine rings. She picked one.

I asked, "How much does that ring cost?"

"Commandante you cannot spend any money in my store. It would be a pleasure to make it a gift for your beautiful daughter."

"Thank you very much. However I cannot accept a gift this expensive."

"I repeat. I will not accept any money from you, Commandante."

He then gave my wife and me each a beautiful ring. I am wearing mine while writing this book.

The Cesar's Palace Hotel is on the beach in Leblon. The hotel serves Feijoada on Saturdays. Feijoada is a dish made of black beans and several cuts of pork, traditionally served with rice, kale, and manioc meal, and always accompanied by a Caipirinha. We often ate the Feijoada in the dining room of the Cesar's Palace Hotel.

Below is a photograph of a pot of Feijoada.

We especially like a nightclub called Plataforma, because of its show. In the Plataforma Show, the audience watches, the largest and most traditional spectacle of authentic Brazilian folklore. The show has rhythms, melodies, songs and typical dances that shows story of Brazil's racial and cultural roots.

For nearly two hours of spectacle, a cast of talented and graceful dancers and drummers are in constant movement and sound, displaying the cultural origins of Brazilian popular music, the result of mixing between Portuguese, Indians and Africans.

The show ends with a parade of costumes in rich colors of the Brazilian flag, the green (of the woods and forests), yellow (gold and riches of the country), blue (the sky and the constellation of Crux) and white (peace), highlighting some important figures of national history.

Below is a photograph of a Brazilian flag.

Finally, an unforgettable program in which the soul of a nation is shown in music and dance for tourists from all parts of Brazil and the world!

Whenever we had guest for visit us from the US, we took them first too the Plataforma for a good dinner and the show.

Below is a photograph of dancers in the show.

The Maracanã Stadium is a large open-air stadium. We often drove by it on our way to the airport. The Rio de Janeiro state government owns the stadium. It opened in 1950 to host the Soccer World Cup. The stadium hosts world famous Rio Carnival. We often drove by the stadium on our way to the international airport.

Pictured below are the Maracanã Stadium and its surrounding middle class neighborhoods.

Samba schools are very large groups of performers, financed by respected organizations (as well as illegal gambling groups). They are for devoted to practicing and exhibiting samba, an African-Brazilian dance. The schools are traditionally associated with a particular neighborhood, often shanty towns ("favela"). Throughout the year the samba schools have various happenings and events, most important of which are rehearsals for the main event which is the yearly carnival.

During Carnival in Rio, Samba Schools perform in the Sambadrome, which runs four entire nights. They are part of an official competition, divided into seven divisions, in which a single school is declared the winner, according to costume, flow, theme, and band music quality and performance.

The performers have to wear a costume. Most of the performers receive their costumes free from being part of the community or pay a small amount for it.

Below is a photograph of the Samba School Parade.

I was often offered expensive Samba Parade tickets. However, I did not think the parade was appropriate for my children even though they were teenagers. The samba dancer wore very skimpy and sexually implicit costumes.

Below is a photograph of a typical Samba School dancer.

Carnival is a festive season that occurs immediately before Lent though out Brazil. Carnival typically involves many public celebrations or parades. Brazilians often dress up during the celebrations, which mark an overturning of daily life. There were street celebrations that we attended wherever we were in Brazil.

Below is a photograph of a Carnival street parade in Rio.

Salvador has large Carnival celebrations, including typical Bahia music. A truck with giant speakers and a platform where musicians play songs of local with a following crowd both dancing and singing.

The party in Salvador is the longest in Brazil, it takes officially 6 days, but the party can take more than 12 days. It is known as the biggest popular party of the world.

Below is a photograph of a street parade we watched in Salvador.

Barra da Tijuca is a famous borough in Rio de Janeiro, Brazil, located southwest of the city on the Atlantic Ocean.

We enjoyed frequenting Barra because of its clean beaches, large number of lakes and rivers, and highly Americanized lifestyle. Barra da Tijuca was built only 10 years before we arrived in Rio. Its streets follow the American standards with large boulevards.

Below is a Photograph of the Barra da Tijuca region.

We often went to the beach at Recreio dos Bandeirantes in Barra da Tijuca region. Recreio has no skyscrapers, and the area contains jungles atop rocky cliffs and hills. High waves permit surfing at Recreio Beach and the white sand beach is used by beach volleyball players. It is about one hour from one half hour from Rio. Most of the people living there are middle-class and high middle-class families, who moved in trying to escape the growing violence of Rio city streets.

Below is a photo of the Recreio Beach.

Below is a Photograph of a typical city boulevard in Recreio dos Bandeirantes.

Chapter 6: Crime in Rio

When we arrived in Rio, the street crime was widespread. However, the longer we stayed, the crime rate kept growing. This was due primarily due the crowding of 9 million people into an area that could only support 2 million people. There were a lot more people than the jobs available for them. Eighty percent of the people in Rio were living in poverty. The police tried to keep the tourist and upper class living areas free of crime, but it was just too much for them.

Tourists were the targets of much of the violent crime. Two thugs killed German tourist for his camera near our apartment. My family took several measures to avoid being mugged and robbed. I never left home without one of my .45s. We dressed as casually as possible, more in the style of regular Brazilians than Americans. We tried not to speak English out in the open. We often walked with me speaking Portuguese to my family. They could not understand most of what I said. They would just smile and say things like yes and no.

We all carried what we called throwaway wallets that contained expired credit cards and other papers and a small amount of Brazilian money. If we were robbed, we planned to just hand the throwaway wallet to the robber and wait for him to run off. Luckily, none of us had to use the wallets.

I kept trying to get the Consul General to allow us to report the serious crime wave in Rio and get the State Department to issue a

Travel Advisory for Rio. He like, many career Foreign Service Offices with the State Department, lived up to the rules of, "Don't rock the boat if you don't have to." and "Don't do anything today that you can put off until tomorrow." I was used to the military way of doing things and never did fully adapt to working with the State Department. The members of the CIA in the Consulate felt the same way about the State Department.

Things finally came to a boiling plate when a female First Class Petty Intelligence Office was robbed in her own home. The robbers broke into her apartment when she was in the shower. When she confronted them, they tied her to a chair, completely naked and scared out of her mind. The robber took everything they could from her apartment, including the TV, Stereo, dishes, and cookware and loaded it into her car. Then they drove away with the car full of what they had stolen. The Petty Office finally worked her bonds loose and called me. She lived close to the Consulate, so had the Marine Gunnery Sergeant lead a team of fully armed Marines to her apartment. All the Marine were hoping the robbers had forgotten something and would come back. I had the Gunny take her to one the best hotels in Rio. He left one of the Marines there until she felt safe enough to be alone.

The first thing I did then was to go to my office, call the Bureau of Naval Personnel, and have them send emergency orders for the Petty Officer to return to the US. She left Brazil on a United America flight to Miami the next day.

I then drafted a complete message to the Director of the Defense Intellect Agency describing what had happened. I described the crime wave in Rio. I stated that I had pleaded with the Consul General to report the situation to the State Department. I requested that the DIA contact the State Department and request them to issue a Travel

Advisory about the crime in Rio. I even wrote what the Travel Advisory should say. The Consul General was in Brasilia for a meeting with the Ambassador. Messages, like the one I wrote, needed to be coordinated with the State Department staff. Since the Consul General was not in the Consulate, I took the message to his Deputy.

The Deputy Consul General read the message and said, "Damn Bruce. I could not have written it any better. You need to send this out ASAP."

When the Consul General returned and read the sent message. He called me to his office. He was obviously very angry and asked, "Bruce why did you send this message without my approval?"

"You were in Brasilia and I thought it was an emergency and the message need to be sent ASAP. I had your Deputy read it and he told me he was OK with me sending it.

He huffed, and puffed and said, "I still wish you would have waited for me to approve."

"You and I both know you would not have approved it."

I walked out of his office without saying another word.

Later, the State Department issued a Travel Advisory, warning US citizens about the crime problems in Rio. The Governor of the state of Rio de Janeiro became involved and provided funds to increase the size of the Rio Police Force. Eventually, Rio became safer for tourists and the State Department rescinded the Travel Advisory. I understand that Rio is much safer today for tourists.

Chapter 7: Gregoria

We hired the Atkinson family's cook and maid, Gregoria, the cook, who was from Peru. Gregoria spoke very little English, so we always communicated in Portuguese.

One day, Gloria said, "Commandante Holdt, I can do both the cook's and maid's jobs and save you money." She always called me Commandante Holdt, no matter how hard I tried to get her to call me Bruce.

Below is a photograph I took of Gregoria with flowers I gave her.

"Gregoria, if you think you can handle both jobs, I will let the maid go."

"Thank you, Commandante."

Later, when I hired one of her friends to be my driver and another to sew a wedding dress for my oldest daughter, Marnie, They all started calling me Padron, which translates to "Father." Padron is the highest praise; a Brazilian can give an American.

Gregoria turned out to be a wonderful cook. Karen bought a Brazilian cookbook called *What Is Cooking in Rio*. Karen worked with Gregoria and the cookbook to arrange the meals she wanted Gregoria to cook.

Below is a picture of Gregoria in our kitchen.

Every so often, I would ask Gregoria to cook a Peruvian dish and surprise us. When she cooked a Peruvian meal, she watched us to see if we liked it. We always did.

One day Gregoria ask us if she could put up a Christmas tre for the upcoming holidays. Somehow she found a tree and trimmings.

Below is a photograph of the Christmas tree.

Gregoria asked me if I would order her a knitting machine form the United States. She said she would pay for it. I ordered it for her, and when it arrived, we gave it to her as a gift. She made all kinds of things with it, even a sweater for me.

Chapter 8: Brazilian Navy

My primary job as the US Defense Attaché, Rio de Janeiro, Brazil, was to gather intelligence about the Brazilian Navy and Marine Corps. The Headquarters of the Brazilian Navy and the Marine Corp were both located in Rio near the American Consulate.

LCDR Atkinson, before he left Brazil, introduced me to both the Brazilian Chief of Naval Operations and the Commander in Chief of the Brazilian Marine Corps. Both the Brazilian Navy and the Marine Corps are organized very similarly to their counterparts in the US Navy and Marine Corps.

Vice Admiral Santos was the Assistant Chief of Operations of the Brazilian Navy. He was very pro-American and sought my friendship. He and his wife had spent a good deal of time in the US, traveling around the United States when he attended the US Naval War College in Washington, DC. The both spoke near perfect English.

I invited ADM Santos and his wife to dine at Olympe, a famous French restaurant near our apartment on the Lagoa with Karen and me.

Claude Troisgros is the chef and owner of Olympe. During a previous visit to the restaurant, he had introduced himself to us.

"My name is Claude Troisgros. I am the chief chef and owner of Olympe. Are you North Americans?"

"Yes I am the US Defense Attaché here in Rio."

"I hope you enjoy your meal."

The meal was delicious. We started with frog legs in a wonderful butter garlic sauce and had superb lamb sweet breads with a crème sauce and ended with Raspberry infused Crème Brule for dessert."

I called the restaurant several days before our dinner with Admiral Santos and made reservations for a table in a quiet alcove in the back of the restaurant.

When we entered the restaurant, we were met Claude Troisgros. "Good Evening Commandante and Signora Holdt."

"Senor Troisgros, I would like to Present Vice Admiral Santos and his wife."

"Good evening Admiral and signora. Welcome to my restaurant." He then escorted us to our table. "Bon Appetite."

After a delicious meal, the waiter brought me the check; I realized that I did not have enough cash to pay the bill and had left my wallet at home. I excused myself and went to the front of the restaurant.

Signor Troisgros was standing by the cash register and smiling at me. "Signor Troigrros, Can I speak to you privately?"

"Commandante Holdt, you don't have enough money with you to pay the bill." Is that right?"

"Yes, sir, it is, I will bring it to you tomorrow," I replied.

He agreed, which saved me the embarrassment of having to ask the admiral to pay for the dinner.

I visited General Luís Alves de Lima e Silva, the Commandant of the Brazilian Marine Corps several times in his headquarters near the Consulate. He had also attended the US Navy War College. He spoke fluent English and was very pro-American. I invited him and his wife to dinner at our home.

They arrived an hour later than the time of my invitation. We soon learned that it was considered polite for Brazilians to arrive late for almost every occasion. Major Richter warned me about this Brazilian custom. Dinner was supposed to be 8 PM. However, I warned Gregoria that we would serve dinner about 9:30.

When they arrived, the general handed me his two .45s. They had pearl handles just like the .45 automatics that General Patton always wore.

After we introduced our wives, I invited then to join us for drinks and appetizers on our balcony. Gregoria had set plates delicious Peruvian appetizers of charbroiled skewers of a variety of meats and chilled shrimp cocktails.

I had earlier asked the Generals Aide what the General liked to drink. He told me American whisky. I bought of bottle of Johnny Walker Black whisky at the Consulate's small commissary. I asked Gregoria to bring the General and me too whiskies neat and to bring glasses of chardonnay for our wives.

"Bruce how did you know I like Johnny Walker Black whisky?"

"General you know about attaches. We have secret methods and sources.

I had also found out from the Generals Aide that the General's favorite seafood was badejo, a locally caught fish, similar to sea bass. Badejo was also my favorite Brazilian fish.

Earlier in the day, I walked to our local fish market and bought two fresh badejo fish. When I got home, I filleted the two fish with my filleting kn+ife that I had included with the other kitchen items we had shipped to Rio from the US. I gave Gregoria directions on how to sauté the fillets in butter and how to prepare my favorite caper and garlic sauce to serve with the fish.

When Gregoria served the fish and the General tasted it, he asked, "How did you know I liked badejo Bruce? What is this wonderful sauce?"

"The sauce is made from capers and garlic sautéed in butter. I had it at a restaurant near the consulate where I often go for lunch. The chef gave me the recipe for the sauce. I will write down the recipe and give to your wife. I do not think that as a General you do much cooking.

"You are wrong about that I enjoy cooking as it relaxes me. While I cook, I can get the problems of the Marine Corps out of my mind."

"I do most of the cooking at home in the US. It is a hobby of mine. However, our cook, Gregoria, here does not like me in her kitchen, so I don't do much cooking now."

"I have the same problem at home."

I knew that the Brazilian Marine Corps Recon Force were responsible for protecting the Brazilian National Petrobras Oil Company's oil drilling platforms. Major James Brockman from the US Marine Corps Recon Force was going to arrive in Rio in two weeks. He phoned from the states and asked me to arrange a visit to an oil platform with one his counterparts in the Brazilian Marines.

He was coming to Brazil, because Brazilian Marine provided protection for oilrigs from any kind of possible assault. He was developing plans for our Marines to guard US oil platforms when terrorists threatened them.

"General I have a favor to ask of you. There is a US Marine Major visiting Rio in two weeks. He would like to visit one of Petrobras' oil platforms with one of you Recon Marine officers to learn how your Marines guard plan to guard the platforms."

"I can do better than that. We are planning to conduct a drill that will simulate a terrorist one of our oil platforms. It is scheduled in about two week. I will introduce you to the Commander of our Marine Recon Forces and direct him to include you and the Major as part of the observation party,"

"Thank you General. That is more than I expected."

When we finished our meal I asked, "General, would you and your wife like to join us for coffee and after dinner drinks on our balcony."

"Yes Bruce. It is very nice outside tonight. We would enjoy joining you on the balcony."

While we were on our balcony, the General and I agreed that I would come to his office in two days to meet with the Marine Recon Force Commander and make the necessary arrangements.

On the day of the oil platform exercise, I dressed in a set of Marine Corp cammies that the Commander of the Recon Force had sent me. It was one of his uniforms. He was a LTCOL, so even the rank insignia was appropriate for me. Because of my deep tan and my ability to speak Portuguese most of the Brazilian Marines assumed I was a Brazilian Marine Corps officer.

At zero nine hundred, Major Brockman and I drove to the Marine Corps helipad on the Brazilian Recon Base north of Rio. I had my driver drive us, as we were not going to flown back from the oilrig. I had requested that we ride back with some of the Brazilian Marines. I had not seen the new Brazilian fast attack boats and wanted to get some photograph of them to send to the DIA.

Shortly after our arrival, we boarded a Super Puma Helicopter. The Super Puma is a four-bladed, twin-engine, medium-size utility helicopter by the French Aérospatiale Company.

Below is a photograph of the Super landing on an oil platform.

After the exercise was completed, we climbed down a stairway on the oil platform and boarded on of the Brazilian Navy Fast Attack boat for a ride back to Rio.

Below is a photograph of a fast attack boat.

Later that year, Karen and I were invited to the annual Brazilian Marine Corps Ball. I wore my Navy Dress Uniform and my wife war a beautiful black gown to the ball.

The ball was held the Brazilian Marine Corps Officer Club on the Marine base in Rio. It was a magnificent event. We were invited back each year we were in Rio and enjoyed each one.

Chapter 9: Antonio Ferrer

Shortly after our arrival, LCDR Atkinson introduced me to Antonio Ferrer, a local Brazilian, who was responsible for husbanding all US ships visiting Brazil. This included providing harbor boats to ferry crewmembers ashore from the larger US Navy ships anchored in the bay, arranging fuel for the ships, purchasing all the food the ships needed, and arranging for the piers where the ships would moor.

He asked all of his friends to call him Tony. Soon he became my best friend in Brazil. Tony owned a shipyard in Niterói, a city across the bay from Rio.

Tony owned a small fleet of harbor workboats that served as ferryboats for the visiting military ships.

Below is a picture of one of Tony's harbor workboats.

Tony was a member of the Rio Yacht Club, a very exclusive, members-only club. Tony arranged to make me a member. We could visit the club whenever we wanted to. The Yacht Club had several great restaurants; one specialized in grilled seafood and even a sushi bar.

Tony owned a nice forty-foot yacht, which he had built in his shipyard in Niterói. Brazil has some very unusual tax laws. The building of a yacht from scratch was highly taxed. However if you rebuilt a yacht it was not taxed.

Tony knew where a yacht about the size he wanted to build had sunk. Tony and several divers who worked for him raised the sunken yacht and towed it to Tony's shipyard. Tony had all of the remains of the yacht removed except for the keel board. He built his new yacht using the keel board of the sunken yacht, so that it was a rebuilt yacht, not a new one. He built a tax-free 45-foot motor yacht.

Below is a photograph of Tony's yacht in his shipyard.

Tony moored his new yacht at the Rio Yacht Club. He often took us on day cruises to nearby ports and sometimes-on weeklong cruises north and south of Rio. Tony had a older man that lived on the yacht full time to guard it and to cook all of the meals that Tony and his guests. His name was Pedro.

Below is a photograph I took of Tony and Pedro.

After we moved into our apartment, I would take a bus to work or have my driver drive me to and from home in one of the two official attaché cars. It became apparent that I needed to buy a car for us to use in the evenings and on weekends.

"Tony, where in Rio is the best place to buy a car?"

"Do you like my Ford?"

His car was a Brazilian-made two-door Ford with a big V-8 engine. It looked and drove a lot like a US Ford Mustang.

"Of course I like it; however, I don't think I can afford as nice a car as yours."

"How much are you willing to spend?"

"I can probably go as high as $5,000."

"Sold for $4,000. I have a Ford just like mine in my warehouse. It has less than fifty miles on it. I was able to get a very good deal if I would buy two, so I bought two and the other is stored in my warehouse."

I bought the car, which only had 20 miles on it and was easily worth $15,000. Tony's car was black. The car he sold us was red, which my wife liked better than black. The new car served us well during our three years we were in Brazil. I sole it back to Tony for $4.000 when we left Brazil.

Below is a picture of our car.

When Tony delivered the car to me at the consulate, he said, "Don't look in the glove box until you get home."

When I arrived home, I opened the glove box; to my surprise, there were two .45 automatics with pearl handgrips and a box of ammunition.

Below is a photograph I took of one of the pistols.

From then on, I carried one the .45 whenever we left the house and put the other in the locked glove box of my car.

Carjacking at knifepoint or gunpoint was common in Rio. The .45 made me more comfortable when driving. No one in Rio stopped at a stop sign or red light for fear of carjackers. They just slowed down, blew their horns, and proceeded through stop signs or the red lights. Surprisingly, there were very few car accidents. I did not see a single car accident during our three years in Rio.

Chapter 10: Tony's Aged Cachaça

Tony was a little crazy. He knew that rum was aged in barrels. The barrels are often placed in the holds of cargo ships so that the constant rocking of the ships would age the rum faster and make it taste better. He tried the same thing with cachaça. Tony filled several oak barrels with different kinds of cachaça, placed them in several of his harbor boats, and left them there for a year.

Below is a photograph of some of the cachaça he used.

When Tony opened the first barrel of cachaça, it had a dark golden color and was smooth, great-tasting drink. One evening Tony arrived at our apartment carrying several bottles of his aged cachaça. He handed me the four bottles. Tony had found several of case of antique bottles and I had never seen anything like them.

"Tony these bottles are beautiful. What is in side of them?"

"Karen it is aged Cachaça."

"I have never heard of aged Cachaça. Where did you buy it?"

"I didn't buy it. I made it. I filled several oak barrels with cachaça, placed them in several of his harbor boats, and left them there for a year. Bring us three glasses and we will try it."

"Gregoria please bring us three glasses, the ones we use for Caipirinhas."

When Gregoria returned with the glasses, Tony first filled one and handed it to Karen, filled the next one for me, and the last one for himself. He raised his glass in salute. "You may now taste the best cachaça in the world."

Karen took a small sip. She smiled and said, "Tony this tastes wonderful. I could not possibly drink regular cachaça straight. You ought to make a lot of this and sell it. You would make a million."

"Thank you Karen. I may just do that."

Chapter 11: Bouzios

One day Tony asked, "Tomorrow, I am taking the yacht to Bouzios, a small beautiful village north of Rio. My son John lives there and I plan to visit him to see my new grandchild. Would you and Karen like to come along?"

"Yes. Thank you, Tony."

Armação dos Bouzios often referred to as just Bouzios, is a resort town and a municipality located in the state of Rio de Janeiro, Brazil. In 2012, its population consisted of 23,463 inhabitants. Today, Bouzios is a popular getaway from the city and a worldwide tourist site, especially among Brazilians and Argentinians.

In the early 1900s, Bouzios was popular with the Carioca's high society, who wanted to escape from the chaotic city life of Rio de Janeiro and enjoy over 23 beaches that the peninsula offers.

Today, the peninsula is a travelling site that offers calmness, direct contact with nature and breathtaking views. The west coast beaches offer calm, clear waters while the east coast ones, facing the open sea, are wild and draw surfers and water sports enthusiasts. At night, Rua das Pedras, Bouzios' main street, offers its visitors an active nightlife and a great variety of shopping and restaurants.

We left Rio the next morning and steamed north.

After about an hour, Tony asked, "Bruce, can you see the big rock ahead of us? I am going to steam right at it and then spin the yacht to enter the harbor of Bouzios. This is the only safe way for a yacht this size to enter the port because of the high currents and narrow channel. I wanted to warn you ahead of time because it will look like we are going to run into the rock."

Karen was below deck and came out on the deck. When she saw the rock dead ahead, she screamed, "No!" Tony spun the yacht, barely missing the rock.

After we anchored the yacht, Tony told Karen, "I am sorry I scared you."

Karen smiled and said, "It's OK. You were just Tony being Tony."

Tony smiled, however you could tell he had no idea what Karen had just said. When we arrived and anchored in the small harbor of Bouzios, Tony said, "We will take the rubber dingy ashore. Will you guys go launch it, while I go below and get my present for my grandchild?"

Below is a photograph of me in the dingy.

We launched the tiny boat and paddled ashore.

"Bruce, you and Karen have time for a walk. There is a very nice market down that block with lots of things made by the local Indians."

"OK, when will we see you again?"

"Let's meet at the restaurant right over there. Would seven o'clock be good for you guys?"

"That sounds great. We'll meet you at seven."

Karen and I walked through the market, buying a multicolored woven basket and a Brazil wood-carved toucan.

"Karen, we don't have to meet Tony for an hour, let's have a drink in that bar over there."

I ordered a beer and a Caipirinha, "O Senhor, una birra e una Caipirinha por favor."

After sitting in the shade under a low palm tree for and several another beer and a Caipirinha, we walked to the restaurant.

Below is a photograph of a street in Bouzios.

"Bruce, can I order for you and Karen? I know you like badejo. Karen, they serve a wonderful fish here called badejo, which I think is grouper in English. The chef fillets badejo in butter and serves them with an alcaparra sauce."

"What is an alcaparra?"

"I think they are called capers in English."

"OK, that sounds good to me."

The fish was delicious, and the caper sauce was just right for the fish.

I make the same sauce today and serve it with all ocean fish, no matter how they are prepared.

Recipe for caper sauce: Melt three tablespoons of butter in a small saucepan. Add two tablespoons of thinly sliced garlic and two tablespoons of drained capers. Squeeze half a lemon into the pan. Sauté the mixture until the garlic is golden brown. Spoon the sauce over the fish that you have cooked, and enjoy.

We finished our meal, had a cognac and a double espresso, and walked back to where the dingy was.

"You guys be careful so you don't fall out of the boat."

I climbed into the boat, and immediately the boat spun away from me.

"You guys row back to the yacht. Now that I am wet, I will swim out to it. There is no way I can get back in the boat in the condition I am in."

"OK. See you back at the yacht," said Karen.

"Just have the ladder waiting for me."

I swam out to the yacht. "Thank God I am a good swimmer," I mumbled to myself.

They were waiting with a ladder, laughing at me.

As I climbed aboard, Karen said, "I can't wait to get back to Rio so I can tell the kids about their father's adventure in Bouzios." As it, turns out Karen said this often after various adventures with Tony.

"Don't you dare!" I exclaimed.

Chapter 12: Paraty

Tony told me about a town south of Rio, Paraty, that he planned to sail his yacht to and asked Karen and I to accompany him. Later that week we drove to the Yacht Club, boarded Tony's beautiful yacht, and sailed about 50 miles south to Paraty. When we arrived in the Bay of Paraty, we moored at a small pier.

Below is a photograph of the Paraty and the wharf where we moored.

Tony planned to sleep on his yacht. I had looked in a Brazilian travel guide and had found a hotel that sounded very nice. In the afternoon, Karen and I decided to take a walk to see the town and find our hotel.

We found Paraty to be a preserved Portuguese colonial town located on the Costa Verde a lush green corridor that runs along the coastline of the state of Rio de Janeiro. Portuguese colonizers founded Paraty formally as a town by in 1667, in a region populated by the Guaianás Indians.

The Guaianás people, who lived where the city now stands, called the entire area Paraty. In the Tupi language of the Guaianás people, *paraty* means "river of fish." Even today the Brazilian mullet still come back to spawn in the rivers that spill into the Bay of Paraty. When the Portuguese colonized the region, they adopted the *Guaianás* name for their new town.

Paraty has cobblestone-paved streets throughout the historic Center District. Paraty maintains many of its historic buildings. Much of the architecture of the city has not changed for 250 years or more.

We walked around the streets of Paraty for about an hour, found our hotel, and checked in. We were thirsty and the hotel owner recommended we try the quint little restaurant next door. Neither the hotel nor the restaurant had any signs to indicate what they were.

We put our luggage in our room. We had a nice balcony overlooking the Bay of Paraty. The room was nicely decorated with antique furniture. Most Brazilian hotels have short beds, as the average Brazilian is much shorter than the average American. We were pleasantly surprised to see a large white feather bed.

We walked next door to the small quaint restaurant. The owner, who was very pleased that we had chosen his restaurant.

We ordered two bottles of Bohemia beer, a dark beer brewed by a German brewery in Southern Brazil. It tasted as good as the beers we drank at Oktoberfest in Munich, Germany.

We were on our own. An old friend who lives in Paraty invited Tony to dinner. I asked to look at the dinner menu. The owner of the restaurant brought over the menus.

In the typical friendly Brazilian manner he introduced himself, "Good afternoon my friends, I am Carlos the owner of this restaurant. I heard you speaking English. I assume you are friends from North America."

Brazilians refer to themselves as South Americans and call Americans from the US and Canadians as North Americans.

"Here are the menus you asked to see. However, we have two items that are not on the menu. I have a friend who nets fresh water prawns. I have an ice chest full of live large prawns. I can reserve you some as an appetizer. I also have mullet, caught today. They are swimming in my big fish tank behind the restaurant. When you order them, we net them out of the tank, clean and cook them, and serve them."

"Carlos I am pleased to meet you. I am Bruce and this is Karen.' We do not even have to look at the menu. We would like the prawns cooked, chilled, and served as the first course. Then for our main course, we would like the mullet charbroiled, bushed with garlic infused olive oil, and served with a caper sauce. If you have it, we would like a crème Brule for dessert. We would also like champagne with our appetizer and you best Brazilian Chardonnay with the main course and cognac and espresso after the desert."

"I can see you have good taste Bruce. I have an excellent Miolo chardonnay from a big Italian wine producing family with a history in Brazil dating back in 1897. I also have a nice Dom Pérignon Champagne and a Remy Martin XO cognac.

We do serve Crème Brule. We just picked some raspberries from our garden and plan serve the Crème Brule with a raspberry sauce.

We also received a ship of coffee beans today from a town near Porto Allegre in Southern Brazil. I buy them from a friend who is a coffee producer. Brazilian restaurants purchase all coffee, because it is so good. They are roasting the beans right in the kitchen."

"I wondered where the coffee aroma was coming from. That all sounds perfect."

"When will you arrive so I can reserve you a rooftop table? It is supposed to be very nice tonight."

"How about eight o'clock."

"I will see you at eight. Excuse me. I need to return to my kitchen to prepare for our evening customers. Good Bye."

"Good bye Carlos.

We returned to our hotel, asked for a 7 PM wake up call, and took a long nap. When we awoke, we showered, and put on dinner clothes. Carlos met us at the door and escorted us to a table on the rooftop of the restaurant. There were four tables on the rooftop but all were empty. We had the rooftop to ourselves. The evening was balmy with a refreshing breeze. The sky was clear and the stars were very bright as Paraty is dimly lit at night with just a few streetlights. Neon signs are not allowed in the town.

When we finished one of the best meals we had during our stay in Brazil, Carlos joined us for coffee and cognac. We talked through two cognacs and two coffees. We returned to our hotel about 11 PM and slept late into the morning.

Below is a photograph of our hotel and the restaurant on the right.

We spent the afternoon exploring Paraty and had lunch at a restaurant on the wharf near Tony's yacht. We boarded the yacht in the late afternoon and sailed back to Rio.

Above is a painting of a typical street in Paraty.

Chapter 13: Capri

After the incident with the pirates, on our way to the port of Santos, Tony said, "We need some fuel after the high-speed maneuvering. I have an Italian friend who lives on an island nearby who I have bought fuel from a couple of times. I am going to moor at his pier."

After we moored, Tony said, "I am gong find the owner to find out if he has enough fuel to sell us some."

A few minutes later, Tony and a tall-distinguished older man walked out on the pier. "Bruce and Karen, this is Giuseppe."

"Bon dia, Senhor. Como você?" (Good day Mister. How are you?)

"I am very well. Your Italian is very good."

"I lived several years in Italy in Naples and Roma, two of my favorite cities in the world."

"I agree. There are times I miss Italy a great deal. However, a paradise like this island is not available near Italy. We named the island Capri, after the famous Island near Naples. My family lived on Capri, before coming to Brazil after World War II. Come join us for lunch."

We walked though his home, a large beautiful villa, to a table in his backyard, where about twenty people sitting around a large table. Italian food covered the table. They quickly made room for us to sit.

Giuseppe introduced us, "Toda a gente, ouvir mais antigo cavalheiro é Tony e atraente casal é Bruce e Karen." (Everybody, meet my old friend Tony and the attractive couple Bruce and Karen.)

We sat down and enjoyed a great dinner. After dinner, a maid brought several bottles of Grappa and pitchers of coffee to the table. Grappa is a strong alcoholic drink made from grapes. Grappa is made by the skins, pulp, seeds, and stems left over after pressing the grapes. Originally, it is made to prevent waste by using these leftovers. When I lived in Italy, I often followed the Italian custom of stopping at your local espresso shop in the winter for a grappa and a cup of espresso on your way to work. Italians believe that Grappa wards of the common cold.

I said, "São destinatárias da presente foi o bood comi uma vez que viveu en Italia, no quarto cinco onnos atrás!" (This is the best place we have been since we lived in Italy twenty-five years ago!)

Chapter 14: Mussel Island

Later that afternoon we fueled and boarded the yacht and got underway. Tony told us, "We will moor overnight near a friend's home on an island south of here. He is quite a character. You will really enjoy him."

About an hour later, we moored in a cove of a small island. "You guys put on snorkels and fins. My friend Jimmie is an Englishman. He loves to eat mussels. You will find ropes in the water out ahead of us, hanging from large pilings. The ropes have mussels growing on them. Collect enough for supper for four people. I am going to swim ashore and invite Jimmie out for a supper of steamed mussels."

We put on snorkels, swim fins, and swam out to where Tony said the ropes of mussels were strung between pilings. Karen and I were able to collect large sacks of large mussels. We swam back to the yacht and handed the sacks of mussels to Rodrigues to clean and prepare for our supper.

Below is a picture of the large mussels in my hand.

Tony returned to the yacht with Jimmie, who was a tall, sun-browned middle-aged man who appeared to be in great shape.

Tony said, "Let's all have a drink. Rodriguez please bring four Caipirinhas and some of the nuts I brought from home. You will like the nuts they are cashews and pecans soaked in honey and roasted in a hot oven. They are very crisp and sweet, great with a Caipirinha."

After dinner, I said, "The mussels in the Provençal sauce were terrific. We had them in Brussels in the same sauce, however these were even better, because Karen and I dove down and got them all an hour ago."

Below is a photo of a plate of the mussels in the Provençale sauce.

Jimmie said, "I am so glad you visited me. Even though I live in paradise, I enjoy visitors every now and then."

Tony replied, "We will get underway early in the morning. I want to get to Santos in time to conduct my business and to get out of their before dark. The less time I spend in Santos the better. We will say good-bye now. I will try to return soon for some more of you wonderful mussels."

Karen said, "Jimmie this visit with you was one of the best times we have had in Brazil. If Tony comes back here while we are in Brazil, you can count on us being with him."

All I said was, "Good bye Jimmie. Thank you. Karen said exactly what I was thinking."

The next morning we steamed down to Santos. Tony conducted his business, and we departed Santo for Rio.

Chapter 15: Brasilia

The government occasionally discussed plans for moving the nation's capital city to the territorial center of Brazil. Juscelino Kubitschek became president in 1955, partially on the strength of his promises to build a new capital. Though many people thought that Brasília was just campaign rhetoric, Kubitschek managed to have Brasília built, at great cost. On April 21, 1960, the capital of Brazil officially moved from Rio de Janeiro to Brasília.

Brasília is the federal capital of Brazil and the seat of the federal government. The city is located in West-Central Brazil, in the sparsely populated Brazilian Highlands. It has a population of about 2.5 Million, making it the fourth largest city in Brazil. Brasília is the largest city in the world that did not exist at the beginning of the 20th century.

I had not yet met the members of the Defense Attaché's offices in the US Embassy in Brasilia. I needed to meet with my boss the Naval Attaché, a Navy Captain whose name was Gary Eide, and the Defense Attaché, an Army one star general, whose name was Norman Snustad.

I needed to be officially presented to Ambassador Harry W. Shlaudeman. CAPT Eide had sent me Mr. Shlaudeman's biographical information, so I could prepare for the meeting. He had a very long and impressive career as a Foreign Service Officer. Recently, in 1984, President Ronald Reagan named Mr. Shlaudeman as the President's

Special Envoy for Central America. Later, he was appointed as the US Ambassador to Brazil. After his assignment in Brazil, President George H. W. Bush then nominated him as US Ambassador to Nicaragua. Shlaudeman received the Presidential Medal of Freedom in 1992.

When our flight landed in Brasília, we took a cab to our hotel.

"Karen, what does the city remind you of?"

"That is easy. It looks and feels like East Berlin. It is all stark-ugly concrete buildings."

"I was thinking the same thing. I haven't seen another car or another human being since we landed here."

Below is a photograph of the skyline of Brasilia.

When we arrived at our hotel, I asked the concierge, "O Senhor, where is a good restaurant for the evening?

"Senhor Holdt, it is Sunday. All restaurants are closed. Your only choice is to eat in the restaurant in this hotel."

"Why are the restaurants closed on Sunday?"

"Most of the people who live in Brasília are politicians who fly home on the weekend, so there is no one in Brasília who wants to eat in a restaurant, except you."

He obviously thought this was very funny. I did not.

The next morning, the Assistant Naval Attaché picked me up. "Good Morning CDR Holdt. I am LCDR Mary Darr."

"Good morning Mary. Please call Bruce. I am not hung up on Navy protocol."

On the way to the embassy, Mary said, "You are invited to my home to my house for dinner tonight. Only my husband Daryl and CAPT Eide and his wife, Sally will join us. It will be very informal, a barbecue in our back yard, starting about 7:30."

When we arrived at the Embassy, we passed through a guarded gate and parked the car next to the largest building in the huge compound. We proceeded directly to the Naval Attaché's office.

Below is a photograph of the US Embassy grounds in Brasilia.

As we entered his office, CAPT Snustad said, "Please sit down over by the coffee table. Would like a cup of coffee?

"Yes Sir. That would be great."

"I will get it." Offered LCDR Darr.

"Thank you Mary. Then, please join us."

"Please call me Norm. I feel like we already know each other. We have had a good many phone calls."

"Norm it is then."

"First and foremost, I want to congratulate you on the many intelligence reports you have filed on the Brazilian Navy, especially the ones one the construction of their nuclear submarine. They must really like you."

"I have been able to make many good friends, especially Admiral Santos the Assistant Chief of Naval Operations. He has been to several dinners at my home. He was the officer that invited me to the Naval Shipyard, where they are building their first Nuke sub. He seemed interested in making sure that the US Navy is aware of the progress they are making. He even pointed out things that I should photographs. That is why I was able to get the good shots of the sub I sent you."

"Yes, we immediately sent them to the Defense Intelligence Agency. I expect you will receive a message from them soon, thanking you for your work."

"I have a friend, Tony Ferrer, who is the US Navy's Husbanding Agent for all ship visits to Brazil. You would never know it by talking to him, that he has a Doctors Degree in Mechanical Engineering from the University of Sau Paolo. He has a friend who is a professor at the university and is the head of their Nuclear Science Division. At Tony's request, the professor has invited me to visit the site of University of Sau Paulo's nuclear reactor; they operate for the Brazilian Navy. They are currently training Brazilian Navy officers and enlisted men in the control and operation of a nuclear reactor. If you like I am sure I could arrange an invitation for you to join us."

"I would really like that."

"Tony will be escorting us. I know you will enjoy his company, In addition to the rector visit, Tony plans to show us the city. He plans to host a dinner at the top of the tallest building in Sau Paulo. He is inviting some of the staff at the nuclear reactor site and the senior officers of Embraer the Brazilian National Aircraft Company. We plan to visit Embraer's aircraft manufacturing site near Sau Paulo. I am sure Tony', with his influence there can arrange for you to fly their newest Brazilian Air Force fighter, the Tucano. Tony went to the University of Sao Paulo with the President of Embraer."

"Damn Bruce that would be great! Do you really think you can arrange it?"

"You can count on it. Embraer has Short Tucano alongside a new version redesigned EMB-312G1, carrying the same Garrett engine as the Short Tucano. The EMB-312G1 prototype flew for the first time in July 1986.

The Brazilian Air Force requested Embraer build a light attack aircraft as part of the Brazilian government's SIVAM (Amazon Surveillance System) Project. This aircraft would fly with the R-99A and R-99B aircraft currently in service and would be responsible for intercepting illegal aircraft flights and patrolling Brazil's borders.

The Brazilian Air Force also wants the Tucano as a military trainer to replace the Embraer EMB 326GB Xavante. The Tucano project plans to outfit an upgraded Tucano that will be suited for the high temperature, moisture, and precipitation, for low threat Amazon region environment. It will also be able to operate in night and day, in any meteorological conditions, and able to land on short airfields."

That is very interesting Bruce. Please put it in a message to me and I will immediately forward it to DIA. You know more about Brazilian Military Aircraft than I do. Even though I am the brown shoe Naval Aviator and you are the black shoe surface jock."

"That is because you are stuck in desolate Brasilia and i am in heavenly Rio where all he action is."

"Some people have all the luck. I will make sure your fitness report reflects all you good work."

"Thanks Captain, but we both know that an Attaché job for a Naval Officer is a dead end, unlike the other services. I know I will be assigned back to Washington. I plan to retire when I have thirty years in the Navy.

I made it from Seaman Recruit to CDR. that is good enough for me. I know I have no chance to be promoted to Captain, no matter how good my fitness reports are. I did things my way rather than the Navy's way. It is my fault I was not promoted to Captain."

"I forgot you started as enlisted man. I will probably retire soon myself."

After my meeting with CAPT Snustad, he escorted me to the General Eide's office. "Please sit down over here. I was just enjoying a good cup of Brazilian coffee, one of the few perks that we have here in Brasilia. I would give my right nut to be assigned to Rio."

"It really nice in Rio, but I don't think it's worth that General."

"Please call me Gary. I feel I know you well after reading all your great intelligence reports."

"Aye aye sir, err I mean Gary."

"Bruce if it was not for you and your army mate down there, we would not be getting much intelligence out of Brazil. All we do here in Brasilia is go to parties and try to look busy. I have given up on trying to look busy."

"I don't envy you living here in Brasilia."

"Do you have anything hot coming up?"

"I have filled the Captain in one my upcoming visits to the Brazilian Navy reactor site at the University of Sao Paulo and a visit to Embraer. I am planning to get any invite for Captain Snustad to accompany us on those visits.

I read your report about the simulated attack on the Petrobras oil platform. It was excellent and obviously got to right place in the Marine Headquarters. I am sure you would like to get back to your hotel for a little rest.

The captain said Mary is having you over for a barbecue tonight. Her barbecues are legendary around here. Make sure you see their parrot. I will not tell you what he does I do not want to spoil the surprise you have in store. Good-bye Bruce and keep up the good work.

Captain Eide arranged for his driver to drive me back to our hotel. Karen and I had a drink and discussed my day at the Embassy. Later, CAPT Eide's driver picked us up and drove us to LCDR Darr's home. It was a very nice modern and open Brazilian home.

We joined everyone in the garden and after introductions were made, Mary's maid brought us Caipirinhas. We all sat down and I said, "The General mentioned something about a parrot that I need to see. Daryl, Mary's husband, walked over to the far corner of the garden to a parrot sitting on a small high perch. He put the parrot on his hand and walked back to the part of the garden we were sitting in.

He brought the parrot back and set it down between us. Daryl said, "His name is Sam and he wants to show you his favorite trick."

Daryl took a small rubber ball out of his pocket trick. He tossed it a little ways in front of him. The parrot ran after the ball and pushed it back to Daryl. Daryl picked up the ball and tossed to me.

The parrot walked over in front of me. I tossed the ball a few feet from me. The parrot pushed back in front of me. I stooped and picked it up.

Below is a picture of Sam waiting for me to throw the ball.

I threw the ball again. We kept playing fetch for about five more times. The six time I threw the ball, the parrot ignored it looked up and jumped up in my lap.

Sally said, "Put him on your shoulder. Do not worry. He is house trained."

I put the parrot on my shoulder and after a bit he playfully nipped on my ear. I guess I looked surprised.

"Sam wants a nut," said Daryl.

I picked up a nut from and bowl of nut that the maid had set on a small table between Karen and me and held it up in front of Sam. He squawked a happy squawk and took the parrot in his beak. Every so often, he would nip on my ear and I would give him another nut.

After about ten minutes, I felt something nudging my knee, looked, and was surprised to see a Rottweiler pip looking up at the Parrot.

"His name is Fritz." Mary told me.

Below is Fritz looking at Sam on my shoulder.

The parrot flew away and landed on his perch. "Fritz wants to play with the parrot, but Sam want nothing to do with the dog," said Mary.

"I did not hear him and would not have known Fritz was there, if he hadn't nudged my knee."

"Most Rottweilers are very quiet. They make terrific watchdogs and attack any intruder. That is why we bought him. There nearest police station is two miles away and we were a bit concerned about a possible house burglary.

"I think the food is ready. Let's move over to the table by the barbecue grill and have dinner." The Darr's cook had been grilling meat on long skewers like the ones used in a Churrascaria.

As guests of honor, the cook served Karen first. He brought her a skewer of meat from the hump of the brahma-like beef raised by all Brazilian ranchers. It was Karen's favorite. He returned to the grill and returned with a skewer of chicken hearts, my favorite.

"Bruce you can have the entire skewer. I am sure no one else will eat any chicken hearts."

Everybody nodded their heads in agreement. Therefore, I had the cook push all the chicken hearts on my plate. "Obrigado Senhor, eu gosto as isso muito." (Thank you. I like these very much."

The maid had placed bowls of Brazilian rice, black beans, and several vegetables on the table. For dessert, she served a delicious compote of a variety of Brazilian fruits. We finished steaming cups of strong Brazilian coffee and the maid kept filling small glasses of Brazilian Cointreau for us.

We were all tired from a long day. I hugged Mary and shook hands with Daryl, "Thank you for a wonderful evening. We hope to see you all in Rio soon. Our maid cooks a mean feijoiada. We will have you all over for dinner the next time you are in Rio."

"You can count on it. Good bye Bruce and Karen"

The driver drove us back to the hotel. When we got up in the morning, it was Monday and Brasilia was a hum with activity. We walked around the city and caught our 2 PM flight back to Rio. The plane was nearly empty returning to Rio. However, I knew it was full that morning when it flew to Brasilia from Rio.

We wanted to visit the Cathedral of Brasília (*Catedral Metropolitana Nossa Senhora Aparecida*—"Metropolitan Cathedral of Our Lady Aparecida"). The cathedral is the Roman Catholic cathedral, serving Brasília, and serves as the seat of the Archdiocese of Brasília. It was designed by Oscar Niemeyer, and was completed and dedicated on May 31, 1970. The cathedral is a hyperboloid structure constructed from 16 concrete columns, weighing 90 tons each.

Below is a photograph of the Cathedral of Brasilia.

Chapter 16: Recife Ship Visit

About a month after our trip to Brasilia, I traveled to northern Brazil to arrange various ship visits. I would sometimes go for weeks and speak only Portuguese.

Below is a map of Brazil and the countries surrounding it.

I flew to the northern city of Recife to arrange an upcoming US Navy ship visit. Recife is located where the Beberibe River meets the Capibaribe River to flow into the Atlantic Ocean. It is a major port on the Atlantic Ocean. Its name refers to the coral reefs that are present along the city's ocean shores. The many rivers, small islands, and over 50 bridges in Recife gives it the nickname of the "Brazilian Venice."

The Metropolitan Region of Recife is the main industrial zone of the State of Pernambuco. It exports products derived from sugar cane, sugar and ethanol, electronics, and food. Recife is the most important commercial center of the Northeastern region of Brazil.

On the day I arrived in Recife, I met with the Brazilian husbanding agent for the port of Recife, Miguel Silva. I needed to meet with Miguel to make all the arrangement for the impending visit of two US Navy Destroyers. They were to arrive the following week so I needed to find a hotel.

"Miguel, I need to find a hotel. I will be here for two weeks. I would like a comfortable hotel room with a separate bedroom, a living room, and a small kitchen. I will be entertaining the senior officers from the destroyer and would like the hotel to have a restaurant to cater a small party. I want to invite the Mayor of Recife and his wife, and of course you and your wife, and any other dignitaries you could recommend."

"You are in luck Commandante. My brother owns a hotel with a nice restaurant right in the hotel. It has a penthouse apartment on the top of the hotel with a nice patio, surrounded by a garden. It is right on the beach. Let us walk down to the pier and we can call him from my office to see if the penthouse is available. Because he is my brother and would be honored to have you as a guest. I am sure I can arrange for a discount for you, if the penthouse is available."

His eagerness to help me was typical of most Brazilians I met. They are a kind and gracious people. It was a beautiful sunny day without a cloud in the sky and a gentle breeze from the ocean. I thought, *another wonderful day in Paradise. I could live in Brazil forever, is my wife would not miss her children so much.*

"You are a lucky man today Commandante. The penthouse is available. It was reserved for two weeks, but the reservation was canceled this morning. I got you a great rate of 1,000 reals per day."

One thousand reals were equal to about $90 that week. "Thank Miguel. I will take the penthouse for two weeks. I will drive over to the hotel now, if you will give me directions."

"You can follow me. The hotel is on the way to my home. I was planning to leave early today anyway,

I followed Miguel to the hotel. The hotel was a quaint building of only four stories right on a very clean, somewhat private cove. Miguel introduced me to his brother, Jose. After a quick tour of the restaurant and outdoor bar next a nice pool, I bought a bottle of Bohemia beer, grabbed my luggage, and took the elevator to the Penthouse.

The Penthouse was like a spacious three room apartment, tastefully decorated with elegant furniture of rattan and dark Brazil-wood furniture. The view from the patio was magnificent. I thought, *This will be a great place for the entertaining I needed to do."*

I spent the two days until the ships arrived exploring Recife and its surroundings. I ate the famous Recife Langostinos that are about the size of a small banana. The restaurants in Recife serve the langostinos chargrilled on a bed of Brazilian rice. Three of the langostinos covered my plate.

The langostinos tasted somewhat like the spiny lobsters I had eaten in Mexico but better. I tried several different restaurants. Each claimed to have a different special sauce that they basted the langostinos with as they grilled. The restaurant in my hotel served best langostinos in Recife.

The port of Recife is somewhat tricky to enter with numerous shoal in the harbor. The city had blasted a channel though the reef that ran along the coastline. Because the channel was not marked clearly, I arranged for a pilot for the lead Destroyer. I rode out to the ship with the pilot boat in a harbor boat.

After boarding the destroyer, I introduced the Commanding of the Destroyer, CDR Lloyd Swift, to the pilot. CDR Swift had been my Executive Officer on my first Navy command, the USS Grand Rapids (PG-98). He was the best Naval Office that I ever served with and we remanded great friend for the rest of our lives.

The Destroyers Planned to visit Recife for a week. After the visit, they were participating in a joint anti-submarine warfare exercise with three Brazilian Destroyers and two submarines. The exercise would be under the command of a Brazilian Destroyer Squadron Commander. I helped him plan the exercise and planned to brief the Officers of the two US Destroyers about the planned exercise.

I invited the COs, XOs, and their four Department Heads to a welcome party along with the Mayor of Recife and the governor of the state of Pernambuco. The restaurant catered the party and Miguel found a local small band that played music for my guests. The next evening, the Governor invited the entire wardrooms of both ships to a dinner party at the Governors Palace. It turned out to be a very successful port visit for the ships.

Chapter 17: Aircraft Carrier Visit

A year after the Recife ship visit, the US Navy scheduled an Aircraft Carrier Strike Group visit to Rio. Carrier strike groups comprise a principal element of U.S. power projection capability.

The carrier strike group is a flexible naval force that can operate in confined waters or in the open ocean, during day and night, in all weather conditions. The principal role of the carrier and its air wing within the carrier strike group is to provide the primary offensive firepower, while the other ships provide defense and support.

The aircraft carrier was the USS Nimitz (CVN-68). The Nimitz is a nuclear powered air craft carrier.

Below is a photograph of the Nimitz.

The group also included the USS Ticonderoga (CG-47), a guided missile cruiser. CG-47). A cruiser is a type of warship. The Ticonderoga-class of guided-missile cruisers is a class of warships in the United States Navy. The class uses phased-array radar and was originally planned as a class of destroyers. However, the increased combat capability offered by the Aegis combat system and the AN/SPY-1 radar system was used to justify the change of the classification from DDG (guided missile destroyer) to CG (guided-missile cruiser).

Ticondcroga-class guided-missile cruisers are multirole warships. Their Mk. 41 VLS can launch Tomahawk cruise missiles to strike strategic or tactical targets, or fire long-range antiaircraft Standard Missiles for defense against aircraft or antiship missiles. Their LAMPS III helicopters and sonar systems allow them to perform antisubmarine missions.

Below is a photograph of the Ticonderoga.

The group also included two destroyers, USS Arleigh Burke (DDG-51) and the USS Spruance (DD-963).

In naval terminology, a destroyer is a fast and maneuverable yet long-endurance warship intended to escort larger vessels in a fleet, convoy, or battle group and defend them against smaller, powerful, short-range attackers.

Below is a photograph of the USS Arleigh Burke.

Below is a photograph of the USS Spruance.

A month prior to the strike group visit, a Navy Supply Corps Office from the Ticonderoga, LCDR David Gates, flew to Rio to meet with Tony, who would be the Husbanding Agent for the strike group. We met in my office and discussed all if the arrangements we needed to make to be prepared for the ship visit. We decided that Tony would rent ten passenger buses to shuttle the crew from the harbor to various sites in Rio, where the sailors from the ships could enjoy themselves.

Tony explained to CDR Gates that he would provide as many harbor boats that would be need to ferry the sailors from the carrier to the area where the buses would be located. We decided that would be best to stage the buses at the head of the pier where the three smaller ships would moor, CDR Gates provide the various orders for such things as fuel, food, and other supplies for each ship.

After CDR Gates departed Rio. Tony and I visited the various merchant facilities in Rio who would satisfy the orders CDR Gates gave to Tony. Each merchant greeted us with open arms. Rio had had visits from US Navy ships but never an aircraft carrier.

I was concerned about making sure that visit would be peaceful and not dangerous for the sailors. Tony scheduled a meeting with the Rio chief of police and his staff. The police identified area of the city that should be off limits to the American sailors for their own safety.

I explained that each ship would assign Officers and Petty Officers to serve as Shore Patrol. Shore patrol are service members who provided to aid and security for the U.S. Navy, while on shore. They are often temporarily assigned personnel, who receive limited training in law enforcement, and are commonly only armed with a baton. Their primary function is to make certain that sailors on liberty do not become too rowdy. They also provide assistance for sailors in relations with the civilian courts and police.

The police chief asked me, "Commandante Holdt how many sailors can we expect to be in RIO one each day?"

I explained, "Navy ship usually allow about 75% of their crew to be off the ship when visiting ports. This is an accurate estimate for all the ships, except the aircraft carrier. A large part of the men on a carrier are there to fly, operate, and maintain the aircraft on board. A carrier has about 5,000 people onboard. Of which, I estimate 4,000 men from the carrier will be ashore each day. The other ships will add another 1,000."

"Commandante Holdt I had no idea it would be that many sailors ashore at one time. I will need to increase the number of policemen on duty during the visit. Thank you for coming here and meeting with us."

I planned to visit the carrier to brief them about Rio. On the morning of their arrival, the cruiser and the destroyers tied up on one of the piers in the warehouse district of the harbor. Tony had a boat standing by to take the officers from the ships to the carrier, so I could brief everyone at one time. When we arrived on the carrier were escorted to the one of the large briefing rooms used to brief Pilots and their flight crews on flight plan for the day. There was standing room only, when we got there. I gave the briefing and returned to pier, where the other ships moored. I stayed on the pier until I felt comfortable that we had enough buses, so that the sailors would not have to stand in line for very long to board the buses.

People from all over Brazil had come to Rio to be part of the ship visit, especially young women, who all wanted to meet the US Navy sailors. The exchange rate made visiting Rio, drinking, eating, and partying very inexpensive. Every bar and restaurant would be open all day and late into the night. To the average Brazilian, even the lowest ranked sailor appeared to be rich men.

Rio was like one big party for the week the ships were there. In many areas, the bars had set up outdoor stands to sell beer and other drinks. There were small bands playing along all of the beaches. The visit went by without a hitch until the day before the ships were schedule to depart, when the police arrested one of the sailors. The sailor was a junior deck seaman from the USS Ticonderoga.

I called Tony and asked him to accompany me to the jail. I wanted him, as my Portuguese was good, but I was not trained to discuss legal issues. I wanted to get the sailor out of jail and back to his ship as soon as possible.

Tony said, "Bruce make sure you bring some cash as we may have bribe some people to get him out of jail."

I had some discretionary funds that were available for something like this. I asked Tony, "Will $2,000 be enough."

"I don't think we will need that much, but bring $2,000."

When we arrived at the jail, we were ushered to the office of the policeman who was in charge of the jail, "Captain Lima is out of the office. He said he would return soon. You can wait here for him."

There was only one chair in front of the desk. "Tony you take the chair." I sat on the edge of the desk.

When the Captain arrived, he scowled at me and said, "I suppose you would like to talk to the prisoner."

"Tony said, "Yes we would."

The Captain picked up his phone and touched a button. He said, "Sergeant come in here."

When the sergeant entered the office the Captain said, "Take these men to the cell that the American prisoner is in.

As we walked to the cell, I said in English, "The Captain seems to be angry about something,"

"Yes he probably took you sitting on the edge of his desk as an affront. Some Brazilians believe it is a sign of disrespect to sit on their desks. Don't worry about it. He will get over it."

When we arrived at the cell. I was shocked. The cell was bout ten feet by ten feet. Besides the sailor, there were three other very rough looking men. The cell was filthy with only an open toilet and no place to sit or lie down. It stunk to high heaven.

The sailor was obviously glad to see us. "Can you get me out of here?"

"Why did the police arrest you?

"I could not understand all they said to me. I think the arrested me for beating up a prostitute. I went with her to a hotel room. She told me that she wanted $200, plus the cost of the hotel room. I only had $100. When I told her this, she became very angry. She picked up the phone and called someone. The only word I understood was Policia."

I gave him the $1,000 and left the room to walk to the pier where my ship is tied up. As I was walking out the door of the hotel, the police arrived and arrested me."

Tony said, "That's all we need. Let's go back and talk to the Captain."

On the way back to the Captain's office, Tony said, "Give me $1,000. I think I can convince the Captain to let the sailor go. It is best that you wait outside the office. He will be hesitant to take the money, if you are there as a witness."

Tony walked into the office and closed the door. I could hear some heated words between Tony and the Captain. Soon they calmed down. Tony excited the office.

"Bruce the Captain is having your sailor brought to the front desk. We will wait there and get him back to his ship as soon as possible. I first offered the Captain $500 to release the prisoner. He said he wanted $1,000, but he agreed to $800."

We brought the sailor back to his ship. I asked to talk to the Command Duty Officer. I told him that he should confine the sailor to the ship just to be sure, the police could not arrest him again.

The next day the ships departed and except for the one arrest, it was a very successful visit.

Chapter 18: Attaché Trip

Later in the year, Karen and I joined a Brazilian-military-sponsored trip around Brazil for Military Attachés assigned to Brazil. First, we flew to the city of Salvador, on the northeastern coast of Brazil.

Salvador is the "City of the Holy Savior of the Bay of all Saints." It is the largest city in the northeast coast of Brazil and the capital of the northeastern Brazilian state of Bahia.

Salvador is noted for its cuisine, music, and architecture. The African influence in many cultural aspects of the city makes it the center of Afro-Brazilian culture.

Of all of Brazil, I like the food of Bahia the most. The local spicy cuisine, based on seafood (shrimp, fish), strongly relies on typically African ingredients and techniques. The most typical ingredient is, an oil extracted from a palm tree brought from West Africa to Brazil during colonial times.

Using coconut juice, Bahians prepare a variety of seafood-based dishes, such as Ensopados, Moquecas, Escabeche, Vatapá, and Bobó de camarão.

Below is a photo of a bowl of Escabeche

Below is a photo of a bowl of Vatapá.

Below photo of a bowl of Bobó de camarão.

We would often walk to the various markets in Salvador. We found stands selling typical dishes of the colonial era. The market restaurants served stews and several fried dishes. We also ate at stands located on the beaches, especially delicious crab stews and oysters.

Salvador was the first capital of Brazil and remained so until 1763, when Rio became the capitol. Many buildings in Salvador are at least two and fifty hundred years old and reflect the architecture of the 1700s.

Below is a photograph I took of a street in San Salvador.

The mayor of Salvador hosted the attachés and their wives to a dinner, held in the backyard of the mayor's large home. Several women were located strategically around the lawn. Each woman was cooking one of Salvador's uniquely tasting special dishes. We tried every dish and loved them all.

I did not take a camera to the dinner. However, in the market the next day, I took a picture of a Bahian woman cooking a similar food to what we ate at the dinner.

Below is the photo I took at the market.

From Salvador, we flew north to Recife. We stayed in a hotel along the beach.

Below is a photo I took of the beach and reef in Recife from our hotel balcony.

After lunch, we drove to a small river that empties into the ocean. On the beach were picnic tables and a woman deep-frying tiny shrimps. Karen and I both bought a large plate full of the shrimps and ate them with the crisp shells still on the shrimps.

Sitting next to us were the British Attaché and his wife trying to separate the shrimps from their shells with knives and forks so they could eat the shrimps. It was an impossible task.

"Why don't you eat the shrimps with the shells on them? They are delicious that way." We could not be convince them to eat the shrimps, shells and all.

After lunch, Karen and I drove our rental car to a home that Salvador Dali had lived in.

We had directions to the house; however, the streets did not have street signs. We asked directions to the house, however no one we talked had ever heard of the Salvador Dali House. We finally asked an American woman who gave us the exact directions in English to the house.

The house now was a small restaurant with a swimming pool, where they served lunch and dinner. Karen and I toured the house that was full of Salvador Dali paintings and changed into our swimming suits to take a short swim, before we ate a late lunch.

They severed our lunch next to the pool. It consisted of a sautéed delicate white fish that was perfectly cooked and delicious. We enjoyed our meal and drove back to Recife.

Our next stop was the city of Natal. We landed at the Augusto Sever International Airport. Natal is the Brazilian city that is the closest to Africa and Europe. The airport has flights to many Brazilian cities and operates several international flights.

Natal is the capital and largest city of Rio Grande do Norte, in northeastern Brazil. The city has a total population of one million.

Natal is famous for its beautiful beaches and many tall sand dunes. We stayed a hotel right on the beach, next to the famous sand dunes of Natal. Karen and I checked into the hotel and had a lunch of grilled fish and Brazilian rice.

Below is a photograph I took of the hotel.

Below is a photograph of the beach taken from our room.

We then rented a sand buggy and spent the afternoon racing up and down the sand dunes.

Above is a photograph of our rented buggy and us

Below is a photograph of one of the sand buggies, racing down a sand dune.

Our hotel was so close to the beach that when you looked out at the ocean from our wide balcony, it looked like the hotel was in the ocean. For supper, we ordered small chargrilled langostinos and a chilled white asparagus salad.

We felt so good; I ordered an expensive bottle of French champagne. After dinner, room service brought us a plate of local fruit and a variety of cheeses with a bottle of Cointreau and a large jug of coffee. We spent about two hours eating and drinking while looking out at the beautiful ocean.

Our next stop was Fortaleza, our favorite city in Brazil. Fortaleza translates to Fortress in English. Fortaleza is the capital of the state of Ceará, with a population close to 2.3 million.

We stayed in a hotel, built right on the beach. We selected a spacious one-story cabana that had a grass roof and a wide balcony overlooking the ocean.

Below is a photograph of the beach cabana we stayed in.

The hotel restaurant served a wide variety of seafood, vegetables, and fruits for dinner. Our breakfast, delivered on a large woven flat bowl, included fresh baked breads, cheese, fresh squeezed fruit juices, and a wide variety of local fruits.

We ate lunch sitting on beach chairs. The lunch was charbroiled seafood on individual skewers and fresh fruit with ice-cold beer or Caipirinhas.

Below is a photograph of Karen I took of Karen and some
friends eating lunch on the beach in Fortaleza.

After three days in Fortaleza. It was time to board the bus back to
Natal to catch a flight to Rio, no one wanted to leave Fortaleza.

Karen and I like Fortaleza so much, we plan to return for a month
or two and rent a small hacienda on the beach. If the price is right,
we may buy one and rent it to tourists when we are not there. We are
planning on flying to Rio and driving north to Fortaleza and stopping
at all of our favorite places along the Atlantic Ocean.

Chapter 19: Southern Brazil

Later that year, I proposed a driving trip from Rio south to the border with Uruguay, stopping at various ports to take pictures of the port and any shipyard facilities. Captain Eide talked to General Snustad he approved the trip.

I talked to Tony Ferrer about the trip. He gave me the names and phone numbers of all the port captains along the route I planned to take. He also phoned each Port Captain and asked them to accommodate my requests. I think Tony was well acquainted with every Port Captain in Brazil.

Port Captains in Brazil mange the entire port where they are located. Their office is usually on the largest pier in the port. They control ships' entry into and exit out of the port. They also manage the port's Ship Pilots.

Karen and I departed Rio in a government Volkswagen sedan with Ted and Missy. I allowed Ted and Missy to take pictures of the outsides of the shipyards as we drove by. They had a great time playing spies. It probably avoided my probable arrest for taking pictures of the shipyards as posted signs said "No Photography Allowed." The Brazilian police would never arrest two beautiful blond American children.

Tony called the owners of each shipyard along the coast. He told them that I wanted to visit their shipyards to determine their capabilities to repair US Navy warships. The DIA knew little about these shipyards and had tasked me to obtain descriptions and photographs of each of the shipyards.

The owners of the shipyards were eager to obtain US dollars. The owner of each shipyard escorted me through their entire facility. They provided me written descriptions of the shipyard's capabilities and encouraged me to take all the photographs I wanted.

Our first stop was the port of Santos. It is the largest port in Brazil and possesses a wide variety of cargo handling terminals—solid and liquid bulk, containers, and general loads that I wanted to photograph.

The Santos Port Captain arranged for me to accompany a pilot who would guide the next ship to enter the port. We took a harbor boat to the ship and boarded it. As the pilot steered the ship into the port, I took photographs of the entire harbor.

Below is a photo of the port of Santos.

The next port was Curitiba, where I again accompanied a pilot and took pictures of the port.

Below is a photograph of the Port of Curitiba.

Curitiba is the capital and largest city of the Brazilian state of Paraná. The city's population numbers approximately 1.7 million. Curitiba is a cultural, political, and economic center in the country and in Latin America.

Near our hotel in Curitiba was a restaurant that Tony had recommended. We drove to the restaurant and ordered a deep-fried whole fish as Tony had instructed us to do.

When the owner stopped at our table to welcome us, I told him that Tony Ferrer had recommended the restaurant. He served us himself and set a large fish looked like a flounder on our table. The chef cut it in small squares. Each square was a mouthful.

Below is a photograph I took of the deep fried fish we ate.

The fish was delicious. Both Ted and Missy liked it, which was surprising, as Missy usually would not eat fish. We spent an hour eating the fish and some wonderful desserts and returned to our hotel.

The next stop we made was to the city of Florianópolis, a beautiful modern city. Florianópolis is the capital of Santa Catarina state. It is composed of one main island, the Island of Santa Catarina a continental part and the surrounding small islands. It has a population of .5 million. The city has the highest standard of living and the best quality of life of any city in Brazil.

The economy of Florianópolis is based on information technology and tourism with 42 beaches and is a center of surfing activity.

Below is a photograph of a beach in Florianopolis.

We were hungry for Japanese food and found the Ronin Temaki and Sushi Restaurant. We started with Sashimi and Sushi. I love octopus sashimi and they brought me an extra order of it when I said I like their octopus very much. For our main course, we had Sukiyaki that was prepared and served in the nabemono (Japanese hot pot) style at our table.

Sukiyaki consists of meat thinly sliced beef. The beef simmers with vegetables and other ingredients, in a shallow iron pot in a mixture of soy sauce, sugar, and mirin.

Below is a photo I took of some of the ingredients

Below is a photo I took of the chef cooking our sukiyaki at our table.

We picked the food directly out of the pot with chopsticks, Japanese style. We dipped in small bowls of raw, beaten eggs.

We had eaten in the home of some Japanese friends and the food was very authentically Japanese. We later learned that the largest concentration of Japanese people in the world, outside of Japan, is located in Brazil.

The next stop was Porto Alegre. Porto Alegre is the capital and largest city in the state of Rio Grande do Sul. The city population is 1.5 million inhabitants. Immigrants from the Azores, Portugal, founded Porto Alegre in 1772.

The port of Porto Alegre is large port for exporting local products, especially beef. It is the southernmost port in Brazil, close to Uruguay. I again hitched a ride to a ship entering the port and took many photos of the port.

Below is a picture of the port of Porto Alegre.

In the late 19th century, Porto Allegre received many immigrants from other parts of the world, particularly from Germany, Italy, and Poland. The vast majority of the population of Rio Grande do Sul is of European descent.

Below is a photograph of Porto Allegre.

Soon after Brazil's independence from Portugal in 1822, the first Germans came to Brazil. Settlers from Germany came to work as small farmers, because there were many land holdings without workers. To attract the immigrants, the Brazilian government promised large tracts of land, where they could settle with their families and colonize the region. The first arrived in 1824, settling Rio Grande do Sul to work as small farmers in the countryside. By 1914, fifty thousand Germans had settled in this state.

Many more Germans immigrated to Brazil during and after the two World Wars. There are towns in the state that look like towns in Italy or Germany. Today, the school classes are still taught in German and Italian.

We decided to take an interior route through Brazil back to Rio. We chose a famous route; called the Rota Romântica (Romantic Route) is a scenic tourist route that runs through 13 municipalities located in the mountainous Serra Gaúcha region of Rio Grande do Sul. The strong German influence is in each of these beautiful towns and villages, truly setting the tour route apart from others in Brazil. The Germanic roots are visible in the architecture, gastronomy and in the accent and language of the people, and, of course, in their Nordic appearance.

The first place we visited was a German-settled town, named Oberammergau, in the mountains outside of Porto Alegre. The city has a beautiful typical German styled entrance.

Below is a photo I took of the entrance to the German town.

As we entered the town, a large sign in the middle of town over the main street said in German, "Welcome to Our Town." All the buildings in town looked like they were magically transported from Oberammergau in the German Alps.

We found a beautiful hotel. Our room looked just like the rooms we stayed in when we were in the real Oberammergau, Germany, years before. That evening we went to a German beer garden for dinner.

Below is a photo I took of the beer garden.

The waitress approached and asked in German, "What would you like to drink?" in German.

I replied in Portuguese, "Two beers and two Cokes."

She looked startled and said in English, "I thought you were Americans."

I replied in Portuguese, "We are Americans."

"Americans don't speak Portuguese!" she replied with a frown, and she walked away.

We waited about ten minutes, and when our drinks did not come, I waved another waitress over. "Our waitress forgot to bring our drinks," I told the waitress in German.

"She didn't forget. She is angry with you. She thinks you are Brazilian, teasing her by saying you are Americans." This waitress served us our drinks and brought us a huge platter of a variety of German sausages and sauerkraut.

Below is a photograph of the inside of the Beer Garden.

After Oberammergau, we stopped at Iguaçú Falls. They are the waterfalls of the Iguaçu River on the border of the Brazilian state of Paraná and the Argentinian province of Misiones. The river flows through Brazil for most of its course, although most of the falls are on the Argentine side. Below its confluence with the San Antonio River, the Iguaçu River forms the boundary between Argentina and Brazil.

The name "Iguaçu" comes from the Guarani or Tupi words "y," meaning "water," and "ûasú," meaning "big."

In 2011, the New Seven Wonders of the World Foundation announced Iguaçu Falls one of the seven winners of the New Seven Wonders of Nature. President Theodore Roosevelt's wife once said, "Niagara Falls is like tempest in a teapot when compared to Iguaçú Falls." The falls were an unbelievable sight, like nothing we had ever seen before.

Below is a photograph of Iguaçú Falls.

Below is a photograph of Iguaçú Falls in Argentina.

From Iguaçú, we drove Belo Horizonte. Belo Horizonte is the capital and largest city in the Brazilian state of Minas Gerais, located in the southeastern region of the country. The city has a population of about 2.4 million inhabitants the city features a mixture of contemporary and classical buildings. Mountains surround the city, which built on several hills. There are several large parks in the immediate surroundings of Belo Horizonte.

Below is a picture of some historical building in Belo Horizonte.

Chapter 20: The US Attaches

CAPT Eide asked Karen and me to accompany them on a trip to visit various cities in Brazil, along with LCDR Darr and their spouses. The Navy had provided a small passenger aircraft for the Naval Attachés to use to visit wherever we wanted to go in Brazil.

Below is a photograph of us standing by aircraft at the Rio Airport.

Our first stop was Salvador. We took cabs to the hotel we were staying in and decided to go to dinner.

I recommended a restaurant that was very difficult to find if you had never been there before. I had eaten there before as the guest of a Brazilian naval officer. Since it was a restaurant that seldom had tourists eat there, the prices were very reasonable and the food was excellent.

I suggested we each order an appetizer and then share them. All the appetizers were seafood. I ordered crab, shrimps, oysters, octopus, and squid. The others ordered a variety of other seafood. Soon our table was covered with plates of succulent seafood. We spent over an hour eating the appetizers and did not have room for a main course.

Below is a photograph I took of one of the appetizer plates.

That next evening Karen and I decided to stay in the hotel and order supper from room service. Our hotel was located on a rocky cove, and our room had a balcony overlooking the cove. We ordered room service. A waiter soon arrived with our food and served our dinner on a table on the balcony. Our dinner consisted of a very large lobster, a whole plate of white asparagus salad, a bottle of French Champagne.

Before we left, we went shopping. Karen and I bought several clay pots that the Brazilians use to cook moqueca. To this day, we use the pots to cook moqueca.

Below is a picture of moqueca cooking in one of our clay pots.

Next, we flew to Cuiabá, the capital city of the Brazilian state of Mato Grosso. It is located in the exact center of South America and forms the metropolitan area of the state. The name, Cuiabá, is of obscure South American Indian origin, reportedly meaning "arrow fishing," and alludes to the Bororo custom of using arrows to fish.

We stayed in the home of my Brazilian friend Admiral Santos, who was the Commander of all the Brazilian Navy in the region. Admiral Santos took us for a boat ride deep into the swamps around Cuiabá.

Below is a photograph I took of our boat.

We had an Indian guide who shot several parrotfish with a bow and arrow. We had the fish for supper. The fish had a beak, much like a parrot used to eat fruit.

Admiral Santos's cook charbroiled the fish and then removed all the bones of the fish and served us all fillets of parrotfish. They had a slight hint of fruit, which is all they eat.

Below is a photo I took of a Brazilian parrotfish, showing it beaklike mouth.

After a long evening of eating and drinking, we retired to our beds for a good night's sleep. Karen and I woke up early and decided to take a walk. I wore my light tan Navy uniform. We crossed over the river and walked into a small village. As we crossed over the river, there were two soldiers manning a checkpoint on the other side of the river. Immediately the soldiers stood at attention and saluted me. I returned their salute however was a little confused about what was going on.

As we walked through the town, people gathered along the sidewalk and stood at attention, greeting me in a language I did not understand. We stopped at a little store to buy woven blanket. The shopkeeper seemed to be very happy to receive American dollars, and I think he thanked me in what sounded like Spanish.

When we returned to Admiral Santos's home, I told him about our experience in the town across the river. He laughed and said, "Bruce, your uniform is identical to what a Bolivian general wears. You were in Bolivia and everyone there thought you were a Bolivian general."

Everyone seemed to think it was funny that I was mistaken for Bolivian General.

Ít would be fun to walk back and see if I could get a free meal at on the restaurant over there"

"I don't thin you would like the food."

Probably not, Admiral. In fact I don't remember seeing any restaurants."

"The people there are very poor. That is why you received such a nice reception when you paid in US dollars.

"It is time we f;y home. Thank you for your wonderful hospitality.'

Thank you for visiting us. We don't get many guests. Good bye."

Below is photo of me in our airplane wearing the uniform
that made me look like a Bolivian General

From Cuiabá, we flew back home to Rio.

Chapter 21: Rio's Restaurants

Rio had some other unique restaurants, besides the ones I have already described. Lord Jim's Pub was the perfect pub to have English tea and to participate in darts championships. It is decorated just like a traditional English pub, with a red telephone booth by the entrance to the restaurant.

Below is a photograph of Lord Jim's.

The pub had posters with various English sayings on them. The good thing about this pub was sampling their large variety of beers and eating the fish and chips, just like the British do.

The evening tea is superb, with traditional scones, muffins, mini sandwiches, and a variety of imported teas. The restaurant also served traditional barbecued pork spareribs, the only restaurant in Rio that served these spareribs. We went there whenever we felt like eating spareribs and drinking great British beer.

They also served what they called a Lord's Jim giant onion. Lord Jims was also the only restaurant that served a US style T-bone steak that was very good.

Below are pictures of Lord Jim's T-bone, spareribs, and giant onion.

Rio also had a several Japanese restaurants manned by Japanese expatriates who migrated to Brazil after World War II. Most of these Japanese people operated truck farms in the state of São Paulo. We liked the Koni Store, a Brazilian chain of Japanese food headquartered in Rio. The Koni Store in Ipanema is located just three short blocks from our apartment.

Below is a photograph of the Koni Store.

The Koni Restaurant sells popular Japanese cuisine-based dishes, such as temakis and sushi, temakis, and sashimi.

The first time we entered the restaurant, we knew we were going to like eating there. It was much like the storefront Japanese restaurants I had frequented when I visited Japan. We sat in the middle of the sushi bar on high stools.

Below is a photo I took of variety of sushi the Koni Restaurant served.

Below is a photo I took of the temakis the Koni Restaurant served.

Below is a photo I took of the sashimi the Koni Restaurant served.

I told the sushi chef that I really liked octopus sashimi and wanted to start with an order of that. I was able to finish the plate of octopus sashimi but barely. It was the only thing I was able to eat. On our next visit to the Koni, I ordered a mixture of sashimi.

Below is a photograph I took of my octopus sashimi.

Karen and Missy would not eat raw fish. They asked me to order them each a plate of California rolls that had cooked crab, avocado, and cucumber.

Below is a close up photo I took of two of their California rolls.

My children thought it was funny that the only way we could tell the chef what we wanted was for me to order for them in Portuguese or for them to point at what wanted.

Ted was much like me, he was an adventurous eater and ordered a little of everything. I did not believe he would be able to eat all of the things he ordered.

I said to him, "Ted you will never eat all of that food."

"Yes I will. Just watch me."

I could hardly believe my eyes when he finished everything and then ask, "Can I orders some more Dad?"

Below is a close up photo I took of the food Ted ordered and finished.

We returned to the Koni Store often, as we knew that we would not be able to afford the high quality of Japanese food we ate once we returned to the US. The food was very inexpensive at the Koni Store for us, because of the high value of the dollar in Brazil.

About two short blocks from our apartment was our favorite watering hole in Rio, the Bar Garota de Ipanema (Girl from Ipanema) Bar and Grill. We went there often for an early supper of their special Chicken Passarita dish. They prepared the dish by cutting and entire chicken into small pieces and deep-frying the pieces and serving them covered by deep fried chopped onions and garlic. We probably ate this chicken once a week. The bar served the best draft beer in all of Rio.

Garota de Ipanema was packed in the evening, so we always went there in the late afternoon. It may have been my children's favorite restaurant for a variety of reason, as they were served a beer if they wanted one.

Below is a photo of the Girl from Ipanema bar.

Chapter 22: Yipee Park

Yipee is a park, nearby Rio. It is located high in the mountains. A friend had recommended it to us, so we decided to give it a visit and made reservations at the hotel in the park.

Since Rio is at sea level and the park was about two thousand feet, it was a long climb to the park on very narrow roads. When cars passed each other, one car had to drive to the very edge of the road to allow the other car to pass.

My wife has a strong \phobia of heights, especially when riding in a car. She asked, "Bruce may I drive. I feel really queasy and I think it would be better for me to drive?"

I knew this was coming, so I said, "Of course. I thought you would ask. Wait until I can safely stop."

I drove for about a hundred yards. We came around a corner, and there was a turn out by a stand that was obviously selling drinks and food. It looked like an entire family was working there. They had a charcoal grill that was grilling some kind of delicious looking meat. We stopped for lunch.

I asked jokingly in Portuguese so my children would not hear, "Is that monkey meat?"

"No Senhor, it is pork but we have some monkey meat, if you would like me to grill some."

I thought she was pulling my leg, "No thank you Senhora. Pork will be fine. We would like four skewers."

She handed me the skewers and asked, "Would you like something to drink?"

"Yes we would. What do you have?"

"We have fresh pineapple juice we made today, freshly squeezed orange juice, fresh coconut juice that we serve in half a coconut. Over there my husband is squeezing sugar cane. My daughter is collecting the juice. She add some lime juice and ice for a very delicious drink.

I looked over at the man operation a big machine. He put stalks of sugar cane on a conveyor belt and the sugarcane stalks ran through a metal press like the press on an old washing machine. It squeezed out the juice into a bucket through a spigot. His daughter turned off the spigot and carried the bucket to table with a jar of lime juice and ice. She poured the squeezed sugar cane juice into glasses then added ice and lime juice.

Below is a photograph they used to squeeze the sugar cane for the juice.

"What would everyone like to drink?

"Ted said, "I want the coconut milk. Please ask if they have a spoon so I can eat the coconut meat after I drink the milk."

"Ted there are spoons in the picnic basket."

"My son would like the coconut juice." Reverting to Portuguese.

Missy said, "I want the pineapple juice."

"My daughter would like the pineapple juice Senhora."

Karen said, "I want orange juice."

"My wife would like the orange juice and I would like the sugar cane juice. How much do we owe you?"

"Senhor that will be five reals."

Five reals was about one dollar at the time. I handed her and 20 reals and said, "Please keep the change."

A look of delight crossed her face. It was probably the biggest tip she had ever received. "Thank you very much Senhor. Is your family North American? I understand a little of the English they were speaking to you. However Senhor you must be Brazilian. I do not think a North American could speak Portuguese as well as you do."

"Thank you for the complement. I am also a North American. We live in Rio."

"Enjoy you food and drinks senhor. And may God be with you!"

"Good bye Senhora. And may God be with you also.

We sat at a picnic bench next to their stand and ate our food. I really liked the sugar cane juice.

"Dad this is barbecued meat is terrific. Ask her how she makes it, so we can make it at home."

We finished a food and drinks and while they were getting in the car, I asked, "Senhora my family liked the grilled pork so much, they asked me to get the recipe. Will you tell me how to make the barbecued meat?"

She smiled and said, "It is old family recipe. It is a bit complicated. You should get a pen and I will write the recipe down for you." I got a pen and paper and she wrote the recipe down for me. We still use it to cook various meats on our barbecue grill today.

"Thank you Senhor. Please stop again on your way down the mountain. We are open all day, every day."

We will. Good bye senhora."

We stopped on our way back from the mountain and the food and drinks were even better. They had added grilled plantains to the menu and we all liked them very much.

When we arrived at the park, and to our surprise and delight, the hotel consisted of beautiful small cabins. The cabins were two stories high. The first story was a living room with a fireplace, and the second story was a two-bedroom loft. The cabins had a beautiful wood cathedral ceiling.

Brazil had always been so warm for us. We could not imagine why we would need a fireplace. That evening we found why we had a fireplace.

"Bruce wake up it is ice cold in here. Pleas start a fire in the fireplace.

"OK, I saw a stack of wood outside. I will get some wood and start a fire."

I stepped outside, and to my astonishment, it was snowing. It was the only time; I ever saw snow in Brazil. I picked up several pieces of wood and carried them inside. I started a fire with a match. The hotel staff had put a box of wooden matches on the fireplace mantel. I closed all the windows in the cabin and woke my family up.

"Wake up everyone and come with me outside. I have a wonderful surprise for you. They woke up and got dressed.

As they walked out the door, they all had faces of astonishment and glee. It was obvious that they had missed the winter snows of Minnesota. We even had a quick snowball fight. However, it ended quickly, as there was not enough snow to make a good snowball. When we entered the cabin, the fire had already warmed the cabin up enough so it was comfortable. We all went to sleep and slept late into the mid-morning.

The camp had a large eating hall with delicious meals, served family style. It also had a medium-sized swimming pool. On Saturdays and Sundays, the staff did a Churrascaria next to the swimming pool.

Below is a photograph of the swimming pool.

We sat in comfortable pool chairs and the staff brought us plates of barbecued sausages, lamb, pork, beef, and chicken and some vegetables and rice with black beans. The food was as good as the best Churrascarias serve in Rio.

At breakfast the next morning, the hotel manager approached our table and said, "Senhor, you and your family should take a walk to a bridge nearby to see our famous butterflies."

"Thank you Senhor. We will take you up on your recommendation." I was not too excited about seeing butterflies but went along with my family to the bridge.

"Dad, these are the biggest butterflies I have ever seen. They are bigger than my hands!"

"Missy, they are as big as dinner plates, and they are of so many colors. I can't believe it!"

Below is a photograph of one of the butterflies that landed on a plant nearby.

We stood on the bridge and watched several Brazilians who were trying to catch the butterflies.

"Dad I wish we had a net. But the Brazilians are not being very successful."

We watched the beautiful butterflies for about an hour. I said, "Let's head back to the camp. I saw a sign that pointed up the mountain that said waterfalls. Let follow the trail and see if we can find the waterfalls."

We walked back towards the hotel and walked for about ten minutes up the mountain trail. We came to a small clearing. Ted was leading the trail. "Come up here, there is a beautiful waterfall. We joined him and saw one of the most beautiful waterfalls I had ever seen.

Below is a photograph I took of the falls.

The falls were about 100 feet in length with clear water flowing from a small stream. The air was misty and very cool. It was very refreshing after our climb up the mountain.

Missy exclaimed, "The waterfalls are wonderful. There are some of the butterflies flying near the falls. Look up the mountain. You can see it rocky top. It still has snow on it. It is so beautiful!

We wearily walked back to the hotel. We intended to only spend the weekend at the hotel. Missy asked me, "Dad, can we stay another two nights?"

"Sure, however that's all. I have to get back to work."

Chapter 23: Monkey Restaurant

We liked to drive south of Rio to some of the cleaner beaches there. On one of our drives, we noticed a new restaurant along the beach. We decided to try it for lunch.

A monkey on a long leash that was very friendly sat on the ground near the entrance to the restaurant. We stopped and fed the money a banana while he sat on my shoulder.

Below is a photograph I took of the monkey.

We entered the restaurant. Constructed to look like a grass roofed beach hut. The kitchen was in the back and in the front were twelve tables covered with colorful tablecloths. Each table had four rustic chairs of a variety of styles.

When we sat down, a waiter approached and handed us menus. "Good afternoon senhor and senhora. Would you like something to drink?"

"We both would like Caipirinhas, made with your best cachaça."

One look at the menu and we immediately knew what we wanted. The first item on the menu described the restaurant's specialty of charcoal grilled shrimp, clams, mussels, langostinos, octopus, squid and a variety of fish all grilled on a small charcoal grill on our table.

When the waiter approached and brought us our drinks he said, "I made then Caipirinhas myself, from our best cachaça. Have you decided on what you would like to have for lunch?"

"Please bring us the grilled seafood for two."

"That is the best choice you could have made. We only use seafood that we buy from Local fishermen who catch or net all of our seafood every morning and deliver within an hour. I am sure you will enjoy it." The waiter brought a large bowl brimming with a variety of raw seafood.

Below is a photo I too of the plate of seafood

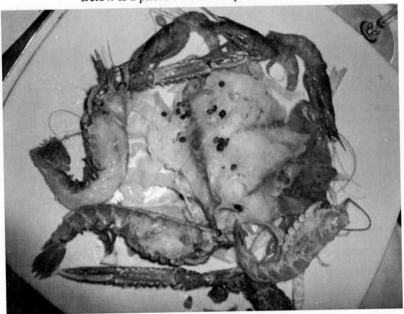

The waiter then brought a small grill that looked like a Hibachi grill with two individual grill racks for each us to grill our own selection of the seafood.

Below is a photo I took of the hibachi grills we used to cook our seafood.

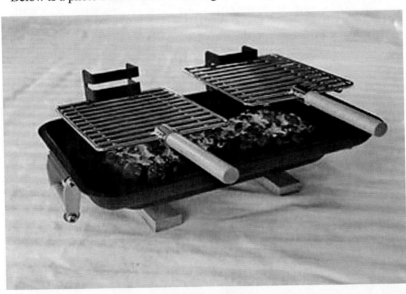

We both selected the seafood we wanted to grill first. As the seafood cooked, we brushed it with garlic infused olive oil. When the seafood was cooked, we ate it right off the grill. When we finished the all of the first grilled seafood, we loaded up the grill with the remaining seafood and ate all of it. The meal was fantastic; maybe our best lunch is Brazil.

We returned to the restaurant often. Once while we were there in the evening, two men carried a large fish through the restaurant to the kitchen. The fish was so fresh that it was still flipping around, so it took the two men to carry it.

That evening, the owner of the restaurant made us coffee in a tall glass globe that was heated, the boiling water ran up to a globe at the very top, and ran down through a long plastic tube to a filter with coffee, and into a detachable pitcher. You used the pitcher was used to pour the coffee into small demitasse cups. She served the coffee with small glasses of Cointreau.

I was so impressed with the restaurant that I wrote an article about it in the consulate weekly newsletter. In the article, I called it the Monkey Restaurant.

The next time we visited the restaurant, the owner put up a big sign over the restaurant that said "The Monkey Restaurant." The bright-lighted sign that was easy to see from the road that ran past the restaurant. She had also had framed my article under glass and proudly displayed it at the entrance to the restaurant.

From then on, the owner would not let us pay for anything we ate at the restaurant as she said my article had caused a significant increase in her business.

Late one evening, as she served us coffee and Cointreau, I asked, "Where can I buy a coffeemaker like this one?"

"I don't know however will let you know later."

The next morning, a messenger delivered a coffeemaker identical to hers, with a note thanking me for writing the article about her restaurant.

Below is a photograph of Karen and me grilling our seafood. The restaurant owner is on the right

Chapter 24: CIA

I had a good relationship with the John Anderson, the CIA Station Chief commonly called Chief of Station (COS), is the top US CIA official stationed in a foreign country, equivalent to a KGB Resident.

In the Rio Consulate, there were three CIA agents: John who whose official title was Director of Cultural Affairs, His wife Virginia whose official title was Assistant to the Director of Cultural Affairs, and Doctor Joseph Benda.

Doctor Benda actually was a medical doctor and he had a small clinic where he provided medical care for the US members of the Consulate. Except the Consul General, I was the only member of the Consulate staff that knew that the three were actually CIA Agents. I could not even tell Karen about them

My friend, Tony Ferrer, came to my office in the Consulate. He visited me often to discuss his preparations for husbanding US Warships that visited ports in Brazil. I could see he was excited and had something important to tell me.

"Bruce you are not going to believe this. The Russian Naval Attaché from Brasilia visited me in my office in Niteroi in my shipyard. There is a Russian submarine coming to Rio. The sub has a burned out generator and must have it repaired. The sub does not have the necessary parts or expertise on board to repair the generator. The

Russian Attaché asked if I could have it repaired in my shipyard in my shipyard. Of course, I agreed."

"Would you help me and John Anderson get onboard the submarine?"

I felt uncomfortable talking to Tony about the CIA presence in Rio. However, I knew he was well aware of who was CIA in the consulate. Nothing got past my friend Tony. He made it his business to try to meet as many of the US staff in the Consulate. John Anderson cover as the Cultural attach fooled most Brazilians but not Tony.

"I would love to help you guys get onboard the submarine. I need some excitement in my life. How about you two acting as my electrical technicians. You can go with me to get the generator and bring it back to my shipyard. I will get you some of my workers coveralls and official looking identity badges like everyone else in the shipyard. You both speak fluent Portuguese and your deep tans makes you look like Brazilians."

"That sounds great. However, I do not think john has any knowledge about the repair of a generator. I sure don't."

"Don't worry I will instruct you on what to do. If we only speak Portuguese, the Russian sailors will not be able to understand us. However, we need to be careful around the Russian Naval Attaché as his Portuguese is pretty good."

"I really appreciate that you will do this for me."

"No problem. I hate the damn Russians. It will give me great pleasure to put one over on them."

Tony loved to use American slang.

"Tony did the attaché tell you when sub will arrive?'

"He said Tuesday morning."

"Good. That gives us three days to prepare."

"Meet me at the Yacht Club at nine, and I will buy you two breakfast. Then we can take one of my harbor boats to the ship. I will have the coveralls on the boat and you can change in route to the anchored sub."

"OK tony, we will be at the yacht Club by nine!"

When Tony left I walked quickly to the Cultural Attaché's office.

"John I have some great news for you but I think we need to discuss it in the safe room." The CIA had installed a room adjacent to John's office that was incased in lead and was swept for any possible bugs, several times a day.

"I will get Virginia, if you think she should be there too."

"Yes that is a good idea. We may need some of her high tech toys for what I am going to invite you to participate in."

"Well Bruce that does sound interesting." John picked up his phone and bussed Virginia. "Dear you need to join Bruce and me in the safe room."

After we were seated at a small conference table in the safe room. I said, "There is a Russian submarine coming to Rio in three days. My friend Tony is going out to the submarine to remove a burned out generator from the sub and take it to his shipyard for repair. The Russian Naval Attaché from Brasilia has requested that Tony remove the generator and repair the generator.

Tony is willing to have you and me accompany him and pose as electrical technicians. Don't worry Tony will instruct you on what to do. If we only speak Portuguese, the Russian sailors will not be able to understand us. We need to be careful around the Russian Naval Attaché as his Portuguese is pretty good."

"Bruce that sound great. Why is your friend taking the risk of bringing us on board?"

"He said he hates Russians. He makes a great deal of money as our husbanding agent and wants to ensure that his contract with the US Navy remains in force as long as possible.

For the last visit of a US Aircraft Carrier with four Destroyers, Tony furnished all the fuel, food, and all other supplies to the ships. He is paid in US dollars for everything he provides the ship. He waits thirty days to pay the Brazilians merchant who furnish him the fuel and supplies for the ships. Besides his markup, he makes a great deal of money, just from the inflation of the dollar.

Tony told me, in confidence, that he made over a million dollars on the last carrier visit. He wants to please the US Navy, so he will do just about anything I ask him."

Virginia said, "Bruce I just received a very small remotely controlled camera the camera is controlled by a small wireless transceiver. We could mount in a cap you could wear while on the submarine. All you would have to do is keep your left hand in your pocket and push the button on the transceiver every time you see something you want to photograph."

"Roger is it OK if I carry the camera instead of you. After all it belongs to the CIA."

"It's OK. You know much more about submarines than I do. You will know better what to photograph. We can make two copies of each photo, one to send to the DIA and one for the CIA."

"Virginia, I will call Tony and have him send over one of the caps his shipyard workers wear and bring it to you today."

"Thanks Bruce. I want to take my time mounting the camera so that it will be invisible to the Russians."

"John's since your last assignment was in our Embassy in Moscow, I assume your Russian is very good. I studied Russian in college but I am afraid my Russian is a bit rusty, as I have not had many opportunities to practice it. I took two years of Russian and the summer between my junior and senior year, I registered for a 15-credit immersion Russian course.

Two close friends took Russian also. They were having many problems and were concerned that they might fail the course. I like diagraming sentences in a high school English class, so I tried it with Russian. I found Russian to be a very logical language, unlike say French. As you know, it is easy to pronounce Russian words if you learn the pronunciation rules.

To make a long story short, I started tutoring my friends every afternoon after classes. After the immersion course, I became relatively fluent.

About five years ago, I was the commanding Officer of the USS Implicit, an ocean-going minesweeper. I was assigned to follow and try to block a Russian military electronic countermeasures trawler who was trying to record the propeller sounds of our new Ohio class submarines as they transited from California to our new submarine base in Puget Sound. I had several opportunities to speak Russian on the radio to the Commanding Officer and my Russian came back quickly.

"Bruce it would be very useful for both of us to be able to listen to the Russian sailors when we are on the sub. Why don't we three only speak Russian for the next few days? Virginia is also fluent in Russian."

"Great idea."

We switched to Russian and spent another hour going over developing a detailed plan of what we intended to do. I had to have them repeat sentences. Eventually my Russian got better and better.

As we were leaving the Consulate on Monday, I said, "John my driver will pick us up at 0800 hours. He can drop us at the Yacht Club before nine to meet Tony for breakfast."

"I don't think there is anything else we can do. I will see you on Tuesday morning. I am very excited about this. It will be a real coup for us if we pull this off."

On Tuesday, my driver us up and dropped us at the Yacht Club. We had a great breakfast of melon and prosciutto, fresh hot French bread with several cheeses and Italian salami, fresh squeezed orange juice, and lots of good Brazilian coffee.

After breakfast, we boarded one of Tony's boats and changed into the coveralls he had brought. John helped me put on the cap and made sure the transceiver was working, so that I was ready to take photographs.

Below is a photo of the yacht club from our boat.

In the red roofed building is the restaurant where we ate breakfast.

"I am sorry that the coveralls are a little tight. You two are big guys. I brought the biggest two pairs of coveralls I could find in the shipyard.'

"No problem do we look like you shipyard electrician?"

"Not yet." Tony said as he handed me a small Tin of grease. "Smear some of that on your hands and a little on your faces."

"Now you look like shipyard workers.

The submarine had anchored on the far side of the harbor as far away from away as possible from Rio and anyone who would try to photograph the sub. It took about a half an hour for our boat to get near the sub. As we approached the Russian submarine, I started snapping photographs.

I exclaimed, "That is an Akula class submarine."

John asked, "What is an Akula."

"The US Navy calls the class, Akula, but is actually the Shchuka class, meaning b in Russian. It is a new nuclear-powered attack submarine class. The first submarine is the Shchuka and first deployed by the Soviet Navy in 1986. The Submarines in the class are very quiet and can reach speeds of 35 knots when submerged and can stay submerged for 100 days. The DIA and I assume the CIA are very interested in finding our as much of the submarine as possible."

"We are really lucky it had problems and stopped in Rio. What is a new Russian submarine doing in the South Atlantic?"

"It was probably in route to Russkaya station, a Soviet Antarctic research station located in western Antarctica. The station was recently constructed. It opened for business in 1980. There are always conducting under water tests. The sub is probably going to the Russian Antarctic Base.

Surprisingly no one appeared to be waiting for us on the deck of the submarine. However, there was a boat anchored on the other side of the sub.

John asked Tony and me "Why do you think the boat on the other side of the sub is doing."

"I think it was probably rented by the Russian Naval Attaché to bring him to submarine so he could interpret for the crewmembers of the submarine.

Tony said, "I think you are right Bruce."

As we steamed closer to the sub, two men stepped out of the sail area and on to the small deck in front of the sail. One was dressed in a navy blue uniform and had four bands of gold on the sleeves of his uniform. I thought, *I think he must be the Russian Naval Attaché from Brasilia.* The other man was dressed in coveralls but appeared to be an officer.

Below is a photograph I took of the Akula class submarine.

The Officer, who I had assumed was the Attaché, hailed us in Portuguese as we approached. "Please approach the submarine, board the submarine, and then have your helmsman, back off. The submarine crew cannot remove the generator. Several of the generators attachment bolts seem to be frozen. Do you have anything that might be able to remove the bolts?"

Tony turned to me and said, "Miguel inside the cabin is a tool box. Get the large cordless electric heavy duty impact wrench and bring it with you on board the submarine."

Luckily, I knew what an impact wrench looked like and was able to find and bring it with me when we boarded the sub.

As Tony stepped aboard, the Attaché said, "This is Captain Third Rank Vladimir Semyonovich, the commanding officer of the Kashalot.

Good. I thought. *We know the name of the submarine is the Kashalot (K-322).*

"It is my great pleasure to meet the Commanding Officer of such a beautiful ship. I would like to present my assistants Miguel and Ademir."

Be careful Tony; don't ham it up too much.

As they escorted us below decks, I handed the impact wrench to John, so that my hands were free to operate the camera transceiver in my pocket. As we entered each compartment of the sub, I would look around and snap photos. Luckily, we walked through the bridge of the sub and I was able to take several photos of it.

When we arrived at the compartment with the burnt out generator, Tony said, "Ademir hand me the wrench."

Tony attached the wrench to one of the bolts and said to me, "Try to remove the bolt. I grabbed the wrench, pulled on the trigger, and held on as tight as I could.

"Good job Miguel. Now try the other three bolts."

I removed the other three bolts. "Miguel and Ademir pick up the generator and let's get it on our boat."

We had not told Tony about the camera in my hat. I was done taking pictures as John and I strained to carry the generator. We finally transferred onto Tony's boat and headed towards the shipyard.

"Tony why didn't you ask the Russians to carry the generator. My back is going to hurt for a week."

"I thought that having you carry it would make sure the Russians thought you were shipyard workers."

It took two days to repair the generator. Several of Tony's workers loaded the generator on the boat and we returned to the submarine. As we approached the Russian Naval Attaché yelled, "The crew will carry the generator on board. After they get it onto the sub, please back off and wait to see if it works, after it is installed."

"Damn." I whispered, "I wanted to get back on board the sub one more time."

Tony waited until we had backed far enough away far enough so that the Russian Attaché could not hear us. "Those bastard Russians don't want us back onboard again. However, I fixed them. I made sure several wires in the generator were loosely attached in areas the crew will not be able to see. In a few days, the generator will burn up again. That will teach them not to mess with Tony Ferrer!"

We had a good laugh and returned to Rio. Virginia developed the photographs I took, and made four copies of each photo. I kept one set. John kept another and we sent copies to the DIA and CIA Headquarters.

About six months later, Dr. Benda arrived in my office and said, "Bruce I need to go to the Manaus. Then, I have get up the river about one hundred miles from Manaus. NSA intercepted a call from the Russian Embassy in Brasilia to Moscow saying that they had heard about a deadly poison that an Indian tribe makes to kill large animals. I need to get there before the Russians do.

Joe continued, "I researched what is known about the poison which is very little. All that I was able to find out is the name of the tribe and that the poison is so potent that in can immobilize a large vicious Amazonia Crocodile."

I replied, "Amazon crocks are very large. It must be a very potent and quick acting poison. What would you like me to help you obtain the poison?

Below is a photograph of an Amazonian crocodile.

"Do you have any contacts either civilian or military in Manaus that might help me?"

"I am not sure let me make some phone calls."

"Thanks Bruce. Call me if you can help."

When the Joe left my office, I immediately called Tony. "Tony this is Bruce, I need some help. I need to find someone in Manaus that can assist me to locate and transport me to a remote Indian village on the Amazon about one hundred miles from Manaus." I had decided that if Benda was going, I was going with him.

"Yes I do. I have a friend who make a living trading with the various Indian tribes near Manaus. If anyone can get you where you want to go, he can. He looks like Pelé, our famous football star, so he everyone calls him Pelé. When do you want to leave?"

I was familiar with Edson Arantes do Nascimento, better known as Pelé. He is regarded as the best soccer player of all time.

"Next week if possible. We could be in Manaus by Tuesday."

"I would like to go with you. However, my oldest son's wife is due to have a baby in the next few days. It is only our second grandchild. My wife would kill me if I were not here. I will call Pelé in a few minutes and get back to you."

Tony called me back in about ten minutes. "Luckily Pelé was in his home in Manaus. He had agreed to take you wherever you want to go. He will meet you on the main pier in Manaus on Tuesday morning. He told me to tell you to bring plenty of US dollars."

I called Joe's clinic and left a message for him to come to my office as soon as he could. When he arrived, I said, "I got your Amazon trip arranged for you. You are to meet an Amazon trader at the Manaus main pier on next Tuesday morning. The trader said to bring plenty of US dollars. If the CIA will fund it and I can get permission from Brasilia, I am going with you."

"I have a large budget for this mission. I can fund an extra person on the trip. I would appreciate it if you would come along. John and Virginia are tied up elsewhere. We can fly to Manaus on Monday."

I wanted to be armed if we were going deep into the Amazon so I drove to a local shop that specialized in making customized leather items and had a shoulder holster made for my 45s and a belt holster for the other. From the leather shop, I walked to an outfitting shop and bought a lightweight safari jacket to cover the guns and matching cargo paints with lots of pockets. Now I felt I was ready for the Amazon.

We arrived in Manaus on Monday evening and stayed in a hotel. We arrived at the pier at 0900 and approached the only boat that looked like the one Tony had described to me. I thought, *are you sure you want to ride it that boat deep into the Amazon jungle. It look like it is lucky to be afloat at all. I am sure glad I can swim when it sinks.*

Below is a picture of the traders boat tied to a pier in Manaus.

Standing on the pier was someone who looked like Pelé. "Good morning. Are you the gentlemen from Rio I am waiting for?

"Yes we are. I am Bruce Holdt and this is Joe Benda."

"I am pleased to meet you. Just call me Pelé. Everybody does. I am not sure I remember my real name. The first things I need to know is what is the name of the tribe you want to visit and what do you want from them?"

Joe replied, "The name of the tribe sound something like Hupdah and we want to obtain their recipe for a poison they make to hunt large animals like crocodiles."

"I am familiar with the Hupd'äh people. I have traded with them and speak a little of their language. I have heard of the poison you are looking for, We had better buy a good deal of trading goods to offer them for the recipe. They will not want to give it to you and will need some convincing."

"The Hupd'äh live in the region along the Negro River near Columbia. As you know, the Amazon River splits into the Negro and Solimões Rivers near here. Look at this map. It is just a simple map; I use to show tourists where I can take them. I do not use it for navigation."

The map of the Amazon River.

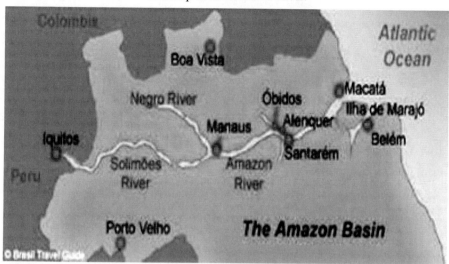

He continued, "While the name Rio Negro means Black River, its waters aren't exactly black. They are the color of strong tea. The dark color comes acid from vegetation in the river's sandy clearings.

The Hupd'äh live on the Rio Negro near the border of Columbia. It will take several days for us to get there so we need to get going as soon as I can buy enough trading goods to get you the poison. Now comes the good part. How much are you willing to pay me?"

"How much do you want?"

"How about $1,000 for my time and extra $500 for the trading goods, supplies, and fuel we will need for the trip?

"It's a deal. Here is $1500. What can we do to help get ready?"

I knew Joe was pleased with the price as he was prepared to pay several times more. Another example of what a dollar could buy in Brazil.

"Nothing. I will take care of everything. Just load whatever you want to take with you on the trip onto my boat. Then get some lunch. I don't have the facilities to cook on board, so we will have to eat what I can buy along with the trading goods."

"What do you recommend we do for lunch?"

"My favorite is the outdoor stand at the foot of this pier. You see the one with the red awning. The owner is a good friend of mine. Her specialty is chargrilled crock steaks. Try them you will like crock."

"Sounds good to me. John lets load our stuff on the boat. I am eager to try the crock steaks."

"OK, but I am not sure I want to eat crocodile."

"I have heard it is very good. It tastes like chicken." I joked.

"You were right Bruce. These steaks are great. The beer is delicious and iced cold."

"I am going to have her pack us some of the grilled steaks to take on the boat. I will buy enough so all three of us can have them for supper. I saw some Styrofoam ice chests for sale near here. While we are waiting for Pele, we can buy a couple and have them filled with ice and beer for the trip."

"Now you're talking Bruce."

We returned to the boat and loaded the beer and food onboard. Then, we sat on the deck of the boat, drinking a couple of beers, while we waited for Pelé to return. When he returned, we helped him load everything on board and departed Manaus.

The area around Manaus had been pretty much be, so except for the heat and humidity, we could have been on a typical large river in the US. However, a few miles up, the Rio Negro the river narrowed some and was bordered by thick jungle. All we could hear was the chugging of the boats engine and the loud jungle sounds. It was my first experience in the jungle and everything around me was fascinating.

I noticed that there were no insects in the air and asked Pelé, "Why isn't there any insect here? There were plenty of them in Manaus."

"The acid in the river water does not allow insects to breed here and kills any that stray into the area."

We enjoyed out diner of crock steaks and cold beer. That night, we slept in hammocks on the main deck of the boat. Surprisingly, I slept like a log and woke up refreshed. Pelé had tied the boat up in a small inlet and had gone into the jungle. Before he left he said, "Build a fire in the sand, I will go see if I can find us something to eat."

Pele returned with a bunch of bananas and a large snake. "This is a small anaconda. I will fillet it into strips can to string on some bamboo sticks and roast in the fire for breakfast."

I had eaten rattlesnake before and knew I would like the anaconda. Joe looked a little green and asked me. "Have you ever eaten snake Bruce? I have not. Does is taste OK?"

"I laughed and replied, "You will like it. It tastes like chicken."

We ate a great breakfast. Joe and I both had seconds.

It took us three more days to reach the Indian village we were looking for. Pele had shut off the motor of the boat. "I do not want to alarm them as they will run away if they don't know it is me. I am going out to the bow and hail them to make sure they know it is me."

When the Indians heard Pele, they gathered at the river's edge and pulled the bow of the boat up on to the shore. It was clear they were pleased with our visit and welcomed us into their village. They talked animatedly to Pele in a language I could not begin to understand.

The crowd of Indians parted, and a tall man who was obviously in charge walked forward and greeted Pele. Pele responded and spoke to the man for several seconds.

"Bruce and John this is the Chief of the tribe. He has invited us into his hut to discuss our business and to have something to eat and drink.

Pele warned me, "Bruce drink that slowly it is a fermented brew of several local fruits. It has a very high alcohol content. Try some of the food and smile whether you like it or not. We must not do anything to to offend the chief it we want to get the recipoe for their poison. I will start the negotiations while you and john sit quietly and eat and drink. Remember keep smiling no matter how bad the things you eat taste. Mark my words as they will definitely taste bad to you."

Below is a photograph of the chief's hut.

I tried some of the food. It tasted awful, but I continued to take small bites and smile, hoping I would not get sick in front of everyone.

Pele said something to the chief who immediately shoke his head in the world-wide gesture that always means no. Pele kept talking and the chief began to smile and eventually seemed to agree with what Pele was saying.

Pele said to us, "The chief has agreed to give you the recipe for the poison, but I had to offer all of the trade gods we brought and to agree to bring him two hunting rifles the next time I return here. That will cost you another $1,000. Rifles are expensive in Manaus."

Jon said, "That a deal then. I will add $1,000 to your payment."

"The only problem is, the Indians can't write down the recipe. They can only show you how it is made. The chief offered to give you all the materials you need to make it so you can bring them back with us."

"Offer him another rifle, if he will guarantee we get plenty of the materials."

Pele muttered something to the chief who immediately clapped his hands and smiled. He obviously liked the idea of the additional rifle.

The chief called several men into the hut and gave them a long string of orders. At least, I think that is what he did.

Pele told us, "The men are going to collect the materials to make the poison and show you how they make it. We will sit here until they return."

About an hour of sitting in the very hot and humid hut, the men returned with an armfuls of different kinds of vergatation. We excited the hut and watched the men as they built a fire, poured water into a earthen pot, and hung it over the fire. Joe was busily writing down everything they did. Everytime they added anything to the pot, they would show Joe exactly what it was and the approximate amount that they added.

After everything was in the pot, they boiled it for about an hour and one of the men dipped a arrow head into the pot. We all walked to the river's edge. About 150 feet up the river, there were several crocks sunning on the bank. The Indian pulled a primitive bow off his back and krept up on the crock and shot it with the arrow. The crock started to crawl into the river, but before it made it into the water it stopped, apparently imobilised by the poison on the arrow. Several women from the village, drug the crock into the village and started butchering it.

Joe removed a glass jar form his pack and handed it to Pele.

Joe said, "Pele please ask them to pour the poison in this jar."

The Indians poured the remains of the liguid into the jar and handed it to Joe.

"At least with this, the CIA will have a sample of the poison in case I didn't get the recipe written down correctly."

Pele said, "You guys load everything onto the boat. I wll give the chief the trading goods I brought and one of my rifles as down payment and we can be off to Manaus. There is still some light left in the day.

The Indians helped us load the materials they used to make the poison. When it was loaded we waved goodby and boarded the boat. In three days we were back in Manaus. The next day we were back in Rio.

When I got back to our apartment Karen, Ted and Missy met me as soon as I got off the elevator and demanded to know all about the trip. I was dirty and exhaused.

"Can't I at least take a shower?"

Ted handed me a large glass of beer, "We are going out on the balcony and you are going to tell us everything thaat happened on the Amazon.

"OK, but it will take an hour or two."

I sat down took a swallow of beer and started telling them about the trip. When I finished, I toke a shower and laid down in our king-sixed bed. I immediately feel asleep and didn't wake until late the next morning.

As I had not had dinner I was very hungry. Gregoria fixed me a large breakfast of thick rare steak, eggs, and hashbrowns, my favorite American breakfast. It was the first time she had prepared such a breakfast. I was sure Karen had helped her.

Chapter 25: The Artist

Missy and Ted attended the American School of Rio de Janeiro with other Americans and children of diplomats and rich Brazilians that wanted their children to learn to speak English fluently.

Below is a photograph of the American School

Rocinha (little farm), the largest favela in Brazil, is located next of the school. A favela is the term for a shantytown in Brazil, most often within urban areas. The first favelas appeared in the late 19th century.

They were built by soldiers who had nowhere to live. Some of the first settlements were called bairros africanos (African neighborhoods).

Built on a steep hillside overlooking Rio, Rocinha, is located about one mile from nearby beaches. Most of the favela is on a very steep hill, with many trees surrounding it. About 70,000 people lived in Rocinha, making it the most populous favela in Brazil.

Although Rocinha is a neighborhood, many still refer to it as a favela. It developed from a shantytown into an urbanized slum. Most of the favela is on a very steep hill, with many trees surrounding it. About 70,000 people live in Rocinha, making it the most populous favela in Brazil.

Below is photograph of the Rocinha Favela surrounding the American School.

Both Ted and Missy liked the school. However, Ted was having trouble with trigonometry. I tried to help him. However, he just did not see any use to learning trigonometry. He finally asked us if he could drop the trigonometry course and take an extra art class. We agreed, and it turned out to be a great choice for him.

Ted and a friend put together a comedy act for the school. They played as if they were a couple of idiots. The Brazilian girls really liked Ted as he was six feet four inches tall, with long blond hair tied in a ponytail. To them he looked like a movie star. Throughout the show, they all chanted "Tedge, Tedge." Since Portuguese does not have the letter *D* in their alphabet, Brazilians pronounce *Teddy* as *Tedge*.

Toward the end of our tour in Brazil, Ted submitted a portfolio of his art to the Minneapolis School of Art and Design, one of the world's best art schools. He also submitted an essay about why he wanted to attend the school. To our great surprise, the school accepted Ted. He attended the Minneapolis School of Art and Design for four years.

Below is a photograph of the Minneapolis School of Art and Design.

His last year of school, he elected, along with a close friend, Sara Mapeli, to travel around the world. The school paid for their transportation out of their tuition and I had to pay for Ted is other expenses. The trip counted as credits for their senior year of school.

They started their yearlong trip, by flying to Greece to stay with a family friend of Sara's. The friend has a villa on a beautiful Greek island.

Below is a photograph, taken from a villa like the one they stayed in.

From Greece, they flew to Berlin, Germany, to stay with a friend Ted had met previously. They were in Berlin when the Berlin Wall fell. Ted still has a piece of the wall.

Below is a photograph of a student tearing down the Berlin wall, while

East German soldiers watched.

From Berlin, they flew to India to stay in a backpacker's hostel in New Delhi.

Below is a photograph of a backpacker's hostel in India.

They both had a bad case of stomach cramps from the Indian food they ate and decided to fly to Kathmandu, Nepal to recover. Kathmandu is the largest urban agglomerate of Nepal. The agglomerate consists of Kathmandu Metropolitan City at its core and its sister cities Patan, Kirtipur, Thimi, and Bhaktapur. Kathmandu metropolis alone has about 1 million inhabitants; and the agglomerate has a population of more than 2.5 million inhabitants.

Below is a photograph of Patan.

They spent a week in Nepal studying the art of making bronze castings in sand.

Below is a photograph of a sand bronze casting in Nepal.

After Nepal, they flew to Chain Mai in northern Thailand to study the art there.

Below is a photograph of the White Castle in Chang Mai.

From Nepal, they flew to the island of Bali in Indonesia to study mask making with a famous mask maker.

Below is a photograph of a mask that Ted carved.

While they were in Bali, Sara became very ill, so Ted flew her to Singapore. The doctors in Singapore recommended that Sara be medevac'd to the United States. Then Ted arranged for Sara to fly to Portland, where her mother lived. Sara had a congenital defect of one kidney, which was removed, and she recovered well. When it was all over, Ted called me to ask if he had done the right thing.

I said, "Ted, you did everything right. I am proud of you."

Ted continued to study mask making for six months in Bali. He then flew to Japan for a short stay and from there back to Portland. He bought a large trunk and filled it full of Indonesian jewelry he had bought in Bali. He sold the jewelry at flea markets in the United States for a good profit.

Below is a photograph of a paining Ted made of a man in Indonesia.

Today, Ted and Sara live in in Washington on the Columbia Gorge and in the mountains of Mexico, where they built, and now operate a six-story tourist hotel. They make their living from selling their paintings and sculptures and from profits from their newly built hotel. You can see my sons art work at www.wilskil.com.

Chapter 26: The Postmaster

After we had moved into our home in Rio, my wife, Karen, was bored, with our kids in high school, and Gregoria doing all the housework she was used to doing. She applied for the position of Postmaster of the US Consulate Post Office. The following is her description of what occurred when she applied for the position of Postmaster.

When I applied for the position of Postmaster, I had an interview with Commander Peter Jones, who was responsible for managing the consulate's infrastructure. It soon became obvious that he did not want a woman running his post office.

He warned me, "There are very strict physical requirements for the job that have to be satisfied, and I do not think you can satisfy them."

"What specifically are the requirements?"

"You must be able to lift that twenty-five-pound package on the floor over there and place it on this table," he replied.

I walked over to the box, picked it up, and set it on the table. "Is there anything else I have to do?"

He replied, "No."

He grudgingly had to give me the job, as he knew my husband would go directly to the Consul General, if he did not. My husband did not think highly of CDR Jones.

I enjoyed being the Consulate Postmaster.

Above is a photo of me at my desk in the post office.

I had two Brazilian assistants that were great to work with.

Once, a three-foot-tall plaster statue of an old-timer sailor fell over and broke in half. It was present I had given to Bruce, so I had to get it repaired. I brought the broken statue into the post office. The post office had a repair bench with all kind of tools.

My assistants jokingly acted like surgeons, glued the statue back together, and painted over the crack so that no one could see that it was ever broken.

I returned the statue to its place beside our fireplace. Bruce was very pleased that the statue had been repaired perfectly. Today the statue sits beside our fireplace in our home in Minnesota and probably ever will as a fond memory of my time in the post office.

Belowis a photograph of the old sailor and his favorite beer.

I continued working in the post office until I returned to the United States to prepare for my daughter Marnie's wedding.

Chapter 27: The Wedding

My oldest daughter, Marnie, was attending Moorhead State University. She was engaged to be married to a dairy farmer who farmed a large farm in Minnesota, near our hometown.

Before their wedding, Marnie and her fiancé, Darrell, visited us in Brazil.

Below is a photograph Darrell took of my family.

Tony took us all on his yacht to Angra dos Reis, a town south of Rio. The town had a nice quaint old hotel.

Below is a photograph Karen took of Tony and me on the bridge of the yacht.

Below is a photo of our three children.

Below is a photograph of the wharf with the hotel in the background.

We anchored the yacht in the bay in front of the hotel.

Below is a photograph of Tony, my daughters and me anchoring the yacht.

For dinner, the first evening, we had a moqueca served on the open-air veranda of the hotel.

Below is a picture of Tony serving me some of the moqueca.

The typical Brazilian is shorter than a US citizen is. Therefore, the beds in hotels, where usually only Brazilians stay, are much shorter than beds in the US. Darrell and Ted, who are both over six feet tall, could not sleep in the beds. Darrell slept on a couch on the balcony of the hotel. Ted swam out and slept on Tony's yacht.

Both Darrell and Marnie were extremely sunburned. Their backs and feet were blistered. Brazil has aloe plants growing just about everywhere along the coast, so we were able to use the aloe plants to squeeze the oil from the plants on the blisters to take some of the pain away. Tony, being a Brazilian, was used to being in the sun and was very tan. He was very surprised that the aloe worked so well.

Before Marnie left, the seamstress that Gregoria had found for us took her measurements to make Marnie's wedding dress. Karen had bought the lace and other materials on a previous trip to Salvador, a city in northern Brazil.

When Karen flew back to the States to help prepare for Marnie's wedding, Missy and I were alone in the in our apartment.

On the weekends, our apartment became her girlfriends' favorite hangout. Many times, I awoke in the morning and found four to five teenage girls asleep in every bed and on our couches.

Missy asked me to escort her to her champagne ball, which is the same as a prom in the United States. She wore a beautiful gown. I wore my white dress uniform with my sword.

We took a limousine to the dance. Missy promptly left me after our arrival to find our friends. I did not mind, as there was a fountain with flowing champagne and a seafood buffet. I stayed at the ball until Missy told me I could leave as she had a ride home.

Below is a photograph of Missy and me before we left for the ball.

Missy and I flew back to the states together for the wedding I wore my full dress uniform to Marnie's wedding. I was very tan from spending so much time on the beach back in Rio.

Below is a photograph from the wedding of Marnie and me.

One young boy approached me while I was in the receiving line after the wedding.

"What country are you king of?" he asked.

"Brazil," I replied.

He stuck out his hand for me to shake and ran off. I later noticed him talking to his mother and pointing at me. She just smiled at me, enjoying the joke.

Below is a photograph from the wedding of our family.

Chapter 28: The Amazon

Karen's sister Joan and her husband, Mathew Macheledt, flew from the United States to Rio. We met them in the airport, and after lunch, we flew to Manaus.

Below is a photograph of Karen on the left, me in the center, and Joan on the right having a drink at the airport,

Manaus is the capital of the state of Amazonas, is located near at the confluence of the Negro and Solimões Rivers. It is the most populous city of Amazonas. The city was founded in 1669 as the Fort of São José do Rio Negro. On the way to our hotel, I saw a beautiful old building. I asked the driver to stop in front of the building so we could take pictures of it. The driver told us that it was the Manaus Opera House.

Below is a photograph that I took of the Manaus Opera House.

The hotel was a very old but modernized hotel.

Below is an aerial photograph of the hotel.

Next to the pool was an outdoor restaurant with several grilled Amazonian fish. My favorite was the parrotfish that I wrote about earlier in the book.

Below is a photograph of the pool with the restaurant on the right.

We took a cab to a market in Manaus. The market had many stands that sold things made by the Amazonian Indians. It also had numerous food stands.

Below is a photograph of Karen, Joan, and me at the market.

From Manaus, we took a boat up the Amazon to a remote area to Ariau Amazon Towers, the largest treetop hotel in the world. The Ariau Towers is on the Rio Negro (Black River), a major tributary of the Amazon River.

Below is a picture of Joan and one of the waiters on the boat.

The hotel consists of seven towers, with all 288 rooms elevated from the rain forest floor by approximately 100 ft. and connected by approximates 5 miles of catwalks.

The hotel has nearly three hundred hotel rooms in various towers, including apartments, suites, and tree houses. Other facilities within the Amazon treetops include two swimming pools, two 134 ft. high observation towers, and a panoramic auditorium for 450 people. There are also restaurants serving regional foods, bars, and convenience stores.

The hotel has various tours available within the forest, such as canoe trips, jungle walks, piranha fishing, visits to native's houses, and observation of nightlife animals.

Visitors can also observe the *Meeting of the Waters*, where the Rio Negro and the Solimões River meet. Because of density and different temperatures, the rivers do not mix. The separate shades of water run side by side for a length of more than four miles without mixing.

Macaws and various breeds of native and non-native monkeys are common around the towers, and provide much entertainment to the tourists.

We took a typical amazon riverboat to the hotel

Below is aerial photograph of the hotel.

The hotel is nestled in a canopy of trees above the Amazon River. Ariau Amazon Towers is the only hotel resort built completely at treetop level in the jungle.

Below is a photo of the hotel rooms from the outside.
We stayed in two the two rooms with the hammocks on the balcony.

Below is a photograph of one of the rooms in the hotel.

The tropical landscape and playful macaws and monkeys surrounded us.

B

Below is a parrotfish we were served for dinner.

After dinner, one evening I left the restaurant with a glass of wine. All of a sudden, there were three monkeys perching on my head and shoulders, dipping their fingers in the wine, and licking it off.

Joan took a photograph of me with the monkeys and called it "Bruce and his three cousins." The only way to get rid of the monkeys was to pour the wine on the floor and leave. The monkeys hopped of my shoulders to the floor and began drinking the wine.

Below is a picture of my three cousins and me.

During dinner, I met a man who was writing an article for a Japanese travel magazine about the hotel. Later that evening, we were enjoying sitting in a hot tub along one of the wooden walkways. A man walked by us and I said to him, "You can tell the Japanese that this is a great hotel." I realized he was a different man when he walked off shaking his head.

Below is a picture of one of the walkways we used to get around the hotel.

We took a small boat up the river with a guide who carried a spear for spearing fish. The guide had an assistant, who steered the boat by the small motor in the back of the boat.

All of a sudden, the guide leaped into the water and climbed back in the boat, holding a small alligator. He held it out to us so we could touch it.

Below is a Photograph of the guide holding the alligator.

A little further on, the guide speared a fish. It was a piranha. The guide showed us its very sharp teeth before returning it to the water.

The guide then gave us each baited can fishing poles, and we caught several piranhas. We floated down the river and fished for about an hour. I caught the first piranha. Then we all caught several. We had a great time.

Below is a picture of one of the piranhas we caught.

Below is a picture of an Indian we saw paddling his boat on the river.

Below is a photograph of us fishing for piranhas. In the back of the boat is our guide. I am on left with the blue hat. My wife, Karen, is on my right.

Below is a photo of Matt and Joan standing on the Amazon River beach

Below is a picture of us returning from the beach.

After four wonderful days at the jungle hotel, we took a boat back to Manaus and flew back to Rio. Matt and Joan stayed with us for several days in Rio. My friend invited us all to lunch at the Yacht Club.

Below is a picture of photograph of Joan, Matt, and me sitting with my friend Tony, on the right, at the Rio Yacht Club.

Chapter 29: Columbia

Towards the end of my assignment in Brazil, I was in a meeting with Consul General, David Rudh, and CIA Chief of Station, John Anderson. Rudh asked, "Isn't there something we can do about the drug trade in northern Brazil and Colombia?"

"I don't know anything we could do," replied the Anderson.

"I think there is something I can try. Karen and I are flying to Panama for medical reasons. While I am there, I can make an appointment with the US Southern Navy SEAL Command to discuss what they may be able to do about the drug trade."

"That is a good idea. Good luck."

Karen and I flew to Panama. We stayed in a beautiful hotel with a swimming pool right outside our room. We took a swim every night before we went to bed.

The hotel was close to the outskirts of Panama City. There were several excellent restaurants where they served char-grilled seafood. I think we sampled every kind of seafood that was available. All were delicious.

On the second day in Panama, I visited the navy SEAL command. I had a meeting with a team of SEALs, a Captain, a Commander, and two Chief Petty Officers.

The SEALs always have nicknames, called war names. They wear no rank insignia on their uniforms when they go into battle. They do this so that, when fighting an enemy, the enemy forces cannot determine the ranks of the SEALs. Then senior officers and chief petty officers cannot identified and become targets for killing or capture. They also hide their real names so if captured the enemy will not be able to identify, locate, or harm their families. The SEAL can thereby try to avoid the release of any information the capturers want to obtain.

"I asked to have this meeting to discuss the problem we are having in Brazil and Colombia. The drug trade is so bad that the drug gangs are killing entire Columbian families. Do you think there is anything you can do?"

The captain said, "I think so. We have several fast-attack boats that are very fast and can reach speeds of fifty miles an hour. They are heavily armed and are perfect for attacking boats that are carrying drugs. We could also use them to insert SEAL teams into the jungle to attack the drug traffickers at their base camps. We would kill as many as we could. However, the boats are in Panama and we have no way of getting them to the Amazon River."

Below is a photo of one of the Navy SEAL fast attack boats.

I replied, "I think I can arrange a navy LST to transport the boats deep into the Amazon River."

Landing Ship, Tank (LST) is the military designation for naval vessels designed to support amphibious operations by carrying significant quantities of vehicles, cargo, and landing troops directly onto an unimproved shores. An LST is a US Navy ship with a large well in the center of the ship that can be flooded to load and unload boats like the SEALs fast-attack boats.

I sent a message to the DIA, explaining my plan on to use the SEALs to interdict the drug trade I requested that an LST be assigned to carry the boats up the Amazon River.

My request was approved, and soon and the USS Tuscaloosa (LST-1187) anchored off the SEAL base in Panama. I was pleased that the Tuscaloosa was the ship assigned to load the boats as I had served on the Tuscaloosa when I was a LT. All the SEALs boats were loaded and transported to the Amazon River along with a large contingent of US Navy SEALs.

Below is a photograph of the USS Tuscaloosa (LST-1187).

I also asked the SEAL Captain, David Rudh, to fly to Rio so we could meet with my friend, the commandant of the Brazilian Marine Corps.

The CAPT Rudh flew to Rio, and we met with the Commandant of the Brazilian Marine Corps and the head of his reconnaissance force. We agreed on a plan of action to combine the Brazilian recon forces with the navy SEAL teams. I left them to create the detailed plans they would need to be successful.

I did not hear anything about the outcome the mission from the SEALs, which is the usual thing with SEAL operations. However, the commandant of the Brazilian Marine Corps told me, "We attacked and killed over a hundred members of the drug gangs. It was a very successful operation."

At the time all of this was going on, a girlfriend of my son Ted from our hometown in Minnesota, Josie Stich, was visiting him in Rio. They thought they were deeply in love, however as is usually the case with first loves, it did not last.

Recently, I was shopping at a grocery store in Minnesota, near our home and met Juan Herrera. Juan was originally from Columbia. He married Josie and is living in a small town near my home in Minnesota.

"Bruce, how are you doing?"

I was still recovering from my compression fractures in my back, but my liver transplant was very successful. I replied, "Pretty good."

"I would like to thank you for what you did for my country, by helping to eliminate the disease that was killing my countrymen. You probably saved my family and me from death."

I was flabbergasted. "What disease are you talking about?"

"The drug trade was nearly eliminated in Colombia by the SEALs and the Brazilian marines you sent to Colombia."

Because of my five years liver disease, my long-term memory was not very good. I did not remember anything concerning what Juan was talking about. I talked to Josie and my wife. They told me about what I had done. Slowly my memory came back and was able to write this chapter.

Chapter 30: Return to Brazil

After I retired from the navy, I became a consultant. At the time, I was working for SRA International, a large technology consulting company located in northern Virginia. One Saturday I was searching the Internet looking for consultants who had placed their resumes on line. We needed to hire several consultant and I was assigned to find some prospects to hire.

I found an add that said, "Do you speak Portuguese? Are you an experienced project manager of large projects? Would you relocate to São Paulo, Brazil, for two years? If so, call this number."

I called the number. "This is Systemhouse. Tony James speaking."

"This is Bruce Holdt. I saw your add on the Internet advertising a position with your company in Brazil, I speak Portuguese. I am an experienced project manager of large projects. I would very much like relocate to São Paulo, Brazil, for as long as you need."

"Can you fly to Toronto tomorrow for an interview?"

"Of course."

I flew to Toronto and had my interviews with several Systemhouse managers. A week later, I was conducting a planning project to reengineer the operating practices of the largest telecommunication company in Brazil called Proceda.

While I was in Brazil, MCI bought Systemhouse. Later MCI went bankrupt and ceased to be a viable company. I had delivered the planning document to the President of Proceda. He liked the document so much he wanted to hire me as a full-time employee.

"Mr. Sanchez, I am not interested in becoming an employee however would be happy to return as a consultant and manage the implementation of the reengineered business processes for Proceda. However, I will need to hire some consultants to assist me."

"Bruce, that sounds good to me."

I needed to form a company to be able to hire and pay the consultants I would need to complete the project. I formed a company we called QMX Support Services with two friends, John Town and Ed Reynolds.

Ed Reynolds and I, along with eight other newly hired QMX consultants, returned to Brazil for two years to complete the project very successfully. I am still in touch with the Proceda project manager. She is now the president of Proceda.

I continued as Vice President of QMX for ten more years, actively managing several large business-reengineering projects. Our projects included reengineering projects for the US Army and Navy, Research in Motion (the company who makes Blackberry smart phones), Fannie Mae, and Freddy Mac.

In 2008, because of my liver disease I could no longer work and prematurely retired. However, I am now ready to go back to work and plan to return to QMX soon. As you can easily see, I have much to thank Brazil for, and that is the main reason I wrote this book.

About the Author

Bruce Holdt is a retired US naval officer. He spent six years as an enlisted sailor, four of which attending the University of Washington as a student in the Naval Enlisted Science Program. On May 30, 1968, he graduated, earning a Bachelor of Science degree. On August 30, 1968, Chief Petty Officer Holdt was commissioned as an Ensign in the US Navy.

Ensign Holdt served as the Antisubmarine Warfare Officer on the USS Taussig (DD-746) from September 1, 1968, to May 30, 1968. LTJG Holdt then attended destroyer school in Newport, Rhode Island. From April 1, 1971, to October 30, 1971, Lt. Holdt served as Operations Officer on the USS Reasoner (FF-1063). Lt. Holdt then served as Combat Cargo Officer on the USS Tuscaloosa (LST-1187) from November 1, 1972, to March 30, 1974.

Lt. Holdt then attended naval postgraduate school, earning a Master of Science degree. From August 1, 1976, to October 30, 1976, LT Holdt served as the Commanding Officer of the USS Grand Rapids (PG-98).

LT Holdt was assigned to the Office of Chief of Naval Personnel in Washington, DC. From September 1, 1980, to December 15, 1982, LCDR Holdt served as the Commanding Officer of the Implicit (MSO-455).

CDR Holdt then attended the NATO Defense College in Rome, Italy. CDR Holdt was then assigned to the Office of Supreme Allied Commander in Mons, Belgium, from May 1, 1983, to August 1988.

CDR Holdt then served as Operations Officer on the USS Nassau until August 30, 1986. CDR Holdt was then assigned to the Office of Chief of Naval Personnel in Washington, DC.

CDR Holdt was then assigned as the military attaché to Brazil in Rio de Janeiro until September 30, 1989. From there, CDR Holdt served in the Office of Chief of Naval Personnel in Washington, DC, retiring from the US naval service on August 30, 1990.

After his retirement from the US naval service, Mr. Holdt worked as a consultant for several firms. Mr. Holdt applied for a position with MCI as a project manager for a reengineering project for MCI Proceda, a communications company located in São Paulo, Brazil. Mr. Holdt worked in Brazil three months before returning to his home in Minnesota. Mr. Holdt formed his own company with two friends, called QMX Support Services. He worked in various parts of the world, including the United States, Brazil, and Europe.

Mr. Holdt retired in 2005, when he contracted liver disease. On December 1, Mr. Holdt received a liver transplant, and today, he lives on a beautiful small lake in northern Minnesota, where he wrote this book.

Edwards Brothers Malloy
Thorofare, NJ USA
March 3, 2014